NOPE

22 Psychotherapeutic Paths to a Healthy „No"

Dr. med. Barbara Gorißen

Imprint:

Dr. med. Barbara Gorißen
Wilhelm-von-Erlanger-Straße 22a
55218 Ingelheim, Germany
www.Praxis-Dr-Gorissen.de
barbara.gorissen@proton.me
Copyright: Dr. Barbara Gorißen 2024; All rights reserved
Produced by Amazon Distribution GmbH
Imprint: Independently published

ISBN: 9798884412385

Author: Legal professional title Physician. Professional title awarded in the Federal Republic of Germany. Holds the specialist title in Internal Medicine, awarded by the Hesse State Medical Chamber following further education and examination. Additional qualifications in specialized psychotherapy, palliative medicine, and emergency medicine were also awarded by the Hesse State Medical Chamber.

Table of Contents

Prologue   9

1. Gaining Time   13

2. Controlling the Mental Cinema   19

3. Mistakes Are Great   23

4. Respect!   31

5. "More Enemies, More Honor"   37

6. The Inner Judge   43

7. The Rotten Apple   49

8. Negotiating at Eye Level   55

9. Safe and Unsafe   65

10. Ask Instead of Mind Reading   73

11. Cultivating The "So What?" Attitude   79

12. Journey into the Past   87

13. Self-Care is Not a Luxury   93

14. Learning to Visualize   99

15. Perfection is the Wolf in Sheep's Clothing 105

16. Count your blessings   111

17. do you talk kindly to yourself?   119

18. "No" is a complete sentence. Really?   125

19: Don't Fear Role-Playing	133
20. Saying "No" Like an Actor	143
21. Crystal Clear Rather Than Indirect	149
22. Motivational Letters to Yourself	157
Closing Words	165
About the Author	167

PROLOGUE

"I have this immense fear of doing something wrong. Of not being liked by other people. Especially by those close to me, but also by more distant individuals, and even strangers.

Because of this, I also have a great fear of saying 'No'. Most of the time, I say 'Yes' even though I really want to say 'No', and then I regret it afterwards. Of course, I'm mad at myself. Who else, right?

When I'm feeling good, relaxed, and content, and suddenly someone suggests that I've made a mistake, or even openly criticizes me, I freeze up inside like a pillar of salt. On the outside, I make sure not to show anything, trying to stay cool and objective."

This quote reflects the thought process so many of us know all too well, more than just a little. It shows the silent resignation in the minds of so many people whose lives could take an incredible turn for the better: If they learn to first recognize their own boundaries and then communicate them.

This book therefore takes you by the hand and leads you through the often quite complex paths of self-discovery and self-assertion. It's a journey where you will gradually learn to say "No" – not out of spite or selfishness, but from a deep understanding of your own needs and desires.

We will explore together how saying "Yes" when we actually mean "No" hinders us, and how by clearly setting boundaries, we can actually create spaces for ourselves. Spaces in which we can breathe, grow, and unfold.

This book offers 22 solid and practical strategies to stay true to yourself without sacrificing harmony with your environment. It's all about finding a balance – between giving and taking, between self-care and caring for others.

In the following 22 vivid chapters, we will delve into the phenomenon of why it's so hard for us to say "No", and how we might overcome this fear.

You will discover that saying "No" is not just a form of self-defense but actually also an act of self-love and respect for your own limits and needs. But it's also an act of clarity and respect towards other people. After all, they will know where they stand with you. And above all: They can rely on your "Yes" being truly a "Yes".

At the end of this journey, you will not only be much better at saying "No" without feeling guilty or afraid of rejection. But you will also develop a deeper understanding and greater appreciation for the powerful word "Yes" –

because every consciously chosen and meant "Yes" to something is also a "No" to anything that undermines your energy and well-being.

So, buckle up for a journey towards more authenticity, confidence, and personal freedom. Welcome to the adventure of saying "No".

Ingelheim, Germany, March 2024

Dr. Barbara Gorißen

1. GAINING TIME

Why do you always let yourself be caught off guard? Try this secret magic sentence: "I'll think about it."

Don't Let Others Put You Under Time Pressure

There's a sales trick so simple and effective that every salesperson knows it. And this trick is: put the buyer under time pressure, and you've got them in the palm of your hand.

"I need your decision right away because I have another interested party, and the negotiation with them is practically concluded!"

Do you fall for it? The likelihood is indeed high. Because even without such external pressure, many people believe that a request made to them must be fulfilled immediately. And of course, a request can never be declined, otherwise – what actually happens then?

This somewhat resembles the classic parenting situation where a parent is tempted to utter the perilous phrase: "I'm counting to three, then something will happen!"

And as the counting slowly, threateningly progresses ("...two ...two and a half..."), it dawns on the parent: this bluff could backfire terribly if it turns out that actually nothing happens at three. The world just keeps on turning, and they've merely lost their credibility.

Luckily, the offspring doesn't know this and usually does what they're supposed to do by "two and three-quarters."

We all probably remember such scenes from our own childhood when we couldn't negotiate things like tidying up our room or doing homework on an equal footing with adults.

When our parents brought up such matters, they weren't requests, and we didn't have the option to simply decline them.

Moreover, it was not only expected that we would carry out the tasks assigned to us, but it was also crystal clear when this had to be done: IMMEDIATELY.

This clarifies where our deep-seated belief comes from, that a request made to us must be fulfilled immediately, and that a "No" is simply not acceptable.

Today, we are adults, but we still carry around a backpack full of experiences we've collected since childhood.

And despite all our maturity and wisdom, sometimes we still react like the child of back then, who believed they had to fulfill every request immediately – and a "No"? That was as rare as a unicorn in the living room.

Viewed in this light, it's probably not so surprising anymore that we feel so easily pressured to have to implement every request immediately. The old pattern of childish obedience is still deeply rooted in us and makes its presence felt as soon as someone – be it a salesperson with a time-limited offer or a friend asking for a favor – knocks on our door.

But here comes the good news: We are no longer the children of back then. And all we need is a short breather to realize this.

We have the ability to pause, reflect, and then make a conscious decision. The key to breaking out of this cycle of automatic reactions is simply to give ourselves enough time to think.

And that's precisely why skilled salespeople try to prevent this and put us under time pressure.

Because it's this brief pause and thus the return to the self-determination of an adult that they want to block.

"I'll think about it."

This simple phrase is the way out of the dilemma and a truly powerful tool in your self-care arsenal.

The next time you're confronted with a request, take a deep breath and say calmly and kindly, "I'll think about it."

This gives you the necessary time to truly evaluate whether you want and can fulfill this request.

It's not about shirking responsibility, but about taking the necessary time to make a well-considered decision. You have the right to set your own boundaries and make decisions that are right for you.

Remember, a "Yes" under pressure often leads to resentment and overwhelm, while an honest "No" or "I need more time to think" preserves your integrity and secures respect from others – and most importantly, from yourself.

Taking this pause does not mean you're weak or indecisive. On the contrary, it's a sign of strength and self-awareness. It shows that we are aware of our own limits and take the freedom to respect them.

The moment we allow ourselves this freedom, we begin to break the automatic link between a request and the apparent necessity to fulfill it. We learn that a "No" can be just as valid and respectful a response as a "Yes" – and that we have the right to use it.

By making "I'll think about it and let you know" a staple of our vocabulary, we gain not only time to think but also space for personal growth. We finally allow ourselves to step out of the shadow of childhood into the light of our own, self-determined adult world.

Thus, the small, obedient child we once were becomes a confident adult who holds the reins of life firmly in their own hands. We become the directors of our own story, in which we have the freedom to say "Yes" when we truly mean it, and "No" when necessary.

2. CONTROLLING THE MENTAL CINEMA

In the theater of our minds, the most dramatic scenarios often play out, especially when it comes to defending our own boundaries. How can we take back control of the script of our lives? Why not conduct a scientific experiment?

Mental Cinema or Reality?

Have you ever caught yourself spinning wild stories in your mind as soon as someone wants something from you?

Suddenly, scenarios unfold where you either emerge as a hero who saves the day (or possibly even the entire world) or as a villain who lets someone down. This is precisely why you find it so hard to say "No." You don't want to be seen as the villain; you want to be the beloved and celebrated hero!

But please understand this: This game is unwinnable. Neither scenario is likely to happen. Because whether hero or villain, this mental cinema is usually far removed from real life.

It's important to realize that not every request made of you will result in a catastrophe if you say "No." Almost always, the fear of consequences is much worse in our heads than in reality.

So, why not experiment with checking whether the fictional stories in your head actually correspond to the outcome of the situation – or not.

This step is absolutely crucial if you no longer want to be guided by unfounded fears. In psychotherapy, this is called a "corrective experience."

You can tackle this by first examining typical situations you find yourself in repeatedly and where you believe that only a "Yes" offers you a way out.

And please do this not just in your head, but very concretely with paper and pencil.

A Scientific Experiment

Approach this with curiosity, objectivity, and structure, just like a scientist would:

1. Observation of the Initial Situation: Recall a situation where someone made a request of you. Got something? Great. Document the situation precisely: What was asked of you? How did you feel? What scenario played out in your head, and how much did it differ from reality? You can judge the latter most objectively by asking people you trust who were present during the situation.

2. Hypothesis: Make an assumption about what might happen if you say "No" in a similar situation next time. Maybe you fear the other person will be angry or disappointed. Or you believe it might lead to a conflict.

3. Experiment: Dare to say "No" the next time a similar opportunity arises. Be as polite and assertive as possible.

Prepare for this step by imagining possible reactions in as much detail as possible: How might the other person react? What do you fear, what do you hope for?

4. Observation of the Outcome: What actually happens after you've said "No"? How does the person react? How do you feel?

5. Conclusion: Compare the actual outcome with your hypothesis. Were your fears justified? Often, you'll find that the reactions are much milder than expected, or that a "No" even leads to respect and understanding. In psychotherapy, this is called a "corrective experience," and it is one of the most effective mechanisms of action.

Don't just nod in agreement; become active and carry out this exercise now! By doing this, you signal to your subconscious that this issue is truly important to you. So important that you're now actually getting up, grabbing paper and pencil, and starting the scientific experiment.

Trust me: This process will help you expose your irrational fears and recognize that saying "No" is not only possible but often also the healthier option for you and your relationships.

It will also show you that you're not responsible for others' reactions. Your task is to maintain your own boundaries and communicate them. It's NOT your job to please everyone.

With time and practice, you'll find that your mental cinema calms down gradually. You'll feel more confident in your ability to say "No" and realize that you're neither a hero nor a villain. Instead, you're simply a person who is increasingly familiar with and respectful of their own boundaries. This way, you gain not only others' respect but also bolster your self-esteem and self-respect. The vicious circle has turned into an upward spiral

3. MISTAKES ARE GREAT

Most people freeze in front of mistakes like a rabbit caught in headlights. Yet, mistakes are nothing but proof that we're learning something new.

Fact: No master has ever fallen from the sky fully formed.

Let's consider how a child learns to walk. Does it just stand up and stride away? Of course not! It stands up, falls down, and then repeats the process over and over again.

Thankfully, the child is not yet an adult. Otherwise, its reaction might be: "Clearly, walking isn't for me. I should just give up. I'm making a fool of myself. My parents can walk effortlessly. And me? Obviously completely untalented. But, well, nothing can be done. I'm just a loser. I give up."

But what's the child's actual reaction? Not a hint of resignation!

Frustration, yes, of course. There might even be a few tears of anger. But giving up? No way!

"It's now or never," seems to be the motto in their little head. Undeterred, the child gets back up and tries again. And again. And again. With each attempt, it becomes better and more skilled.

What Lies Behind the Fear of Making Mistakes

Are you always striving to make a good impression? Then you've probably developed a great fear of making mistakes.

And then you probably also fear criticism, because it would prove your worst fear to be true: once again, not being good enough.

We'll return to this fear in a later chapter. For now, I want to invite you to a change in perspective.

There's a saying: Look at what a person does most often, and you'll know what they're best at!

And there's truth to that. The day has only 24 hours. This means each of us must decide every day how to use those 24 hours.

If someone wants to learn something new — let's say, to play a musical instrument — they have no choice but to allocate enough time for it.

A vivid case example

Imagine two teenagers, Tim and Tom. Both want to learn to play the piano and sign up for lessons with the former pianist, Madame Leson, at the same time.

Madame Leson quickly notices that Tim is a natural talent. He grasps the basics in no time, music comes to him effortlessly in theory and practice, and Madame Leson even suspects Tim might have perfect pitch.

Tom, on the other hand, she can only describe as untalented (in her thoughts, of course, she would never say that to discourage him!). He seems to have two left hands, doesn't have a particularly good musical ear, and tests Madame Leson's patience.

But Tom has something Tim lacks: a burning enthusiasm and love for playing the piano. And he's not deterred by his many mistakes, because what does he have to lose? He can only get better!

Moreover, he loves music, and whether Madame Leson considers him talented or not, he doesn't give it a second thought. He's too busy enthusiastically pounding on the keys, and he's having a blast.

On the other hand, Tim is terribly upset about each of his rare mistakes. "What will Madame Leson think if I make such stupid mistakes?" he thinks frustratedly. "Maybe she'll start thinking I'm not as talented as she thought!" And that irritates him immensely.

Of course, he's highly motivated to avoid mistakes. After all, they spoil all the fun he has with music.

And practicing at home is therefore not enjoyable for him, especially since his parents put a lot of pressure on him. They bought a grand piano for their son, which now stands proudly in the living room, and they expect Tim to practice there for an hour every day, after all, it cost a lot of money, and the piano lessons should pay off!

Tom could only dream of such conditions. His parents don't support his love for music; he pays for the piano lessons with his pocket money.

They didn't buy him a grand piano, not even an electric keyboard. To practice, Tom first cut out a piano keyboard from cardboard and then practiced the movements of his fingers on it for hours every day.

Eventually, he discovered that for a little money, he could get a roll-up electronic keyboard so at least he could hear the tones while spending all day practicing finger positions.

His parents were annoyed by his "obsession with such useless stuff," but his grandparents eventually took pity and gave him a cheap used keyboard for Christmas.

Now there was no stopping Tom. With relentless enthusiasm and joy, he practiced practically all day – he wasn't bothered by his many mistakes, as long as he could make music.

Quiz question: What do you think happened to Tim and Tom two years later?

It's not hard to guess. The talented Tim with perfect pitch has long lost his interest in playing the piano, and his parents sold the grand piano amid great uproar and with many accusations.

Since then, they've constantly told him he's a good-for-nothing, too lazy to practice, and wasted his talent with his laziness.

Tim has since developed a strong aversion to music and learned from the story how terrible mistakes are, how terrible he is, and that he's troubling his parents with his impossible behavior.

His self-esteem has suffered greatly, and he's trying to cope by now devaluing music and musicians (and after a while, all art and artists in general) for engaging in such a useless activity. As if there were nothing more important in the world?

Tom, on the other hand, has long become Madame Leson's best and favorite student. He now plays the keyboard in his school's rock band, which is not at all Madame Leson's preferred genre of music, but she's bursting with pride over her model student who still spends the majority of his day with music.

"Music is my life!" says Tom — and he's become really, really good at it.

What would have happened if he had been impressed by his mistakes and Madame Leson's supposed opinion of him two years earlier?

And an even more interesting question: Could it be that you're so good at saying "Yes" because you've dedicated so much time to this art throughout your life that you've already mastered it?

And could it be that you're not good at saying "No" because you've hardly ever practiced it? How much time in your life have you spent practicing saying "Yes", and how much time practicing saying "No"?

If you really want to learn to say "No" and be as good at it as you are at saying "Yes", then it's time to start catching up on practice. There's a lot to do.

4. RESPECT!

Trying to please everyone leads to a loss of respect. Such overly adaptive behavior signals a lack of identity and results in not being taken seriously.

Do you have to earn respect? No!

I'm absolutely not a fan of the saying "Respect must be earned." If you hear that, run and get to safety! Because in a healthy interaction between two people, mutual respect should always be the unconditional prerequisite.

Everyone should treat you with respect without you having to do something first. If this is not the case, please turn around and leave!

The fact that one can indeed lose this initial grant of respect over the course of an interaction is a completely different matter.

And that's exactly what so many people are afraid of: what if I lose the laurels my counterpart has initially given me once they get to know me better?

Thinking this way indicates a problem with self-worth — and many people have this issue. They believe they can't possibly meet others' expectations.

So, they try to be liked by at least fulfilling the wishes of others, agreeing with them, not angering them with a differing opinion or, heaven forbid, a "No," and best not to stand out at all.

They fear losing respect if others realize how little they have to offer, how inadequate they really are, so they try to placate them by attempting to please.

And ironically, it's precisely by doing so that they lose respect over time. Because those who beg to be liked may get pity but certainly no respect.

The premise is always (!) wrong: Who — besides you, of course — says that you're inadequate, have nothing to offer, or are not even worthy of walking the face of this earth?

Oh, it's not just you saying that, but actually people in your environment too? Then you should change that environment as soon as possible.

Because it keeps you small and breaks you down — and only someone who also doesn't have a good, resilient self-esteem behaves that way, trying to make others feel small to feel bigger themselves.

Do you know what such people are called in psychology? Right, there they are, the narcissists. And they have the same root problem: a very weak self-esteem.

Only their apparent solution is not trying to please everyone, but rather inflating their weak self-esteem like a balloon and bragging everywhere about how great they are - not such a loser like everyone else around them.

Narcissists only seem to have a (too) large self-esteem. In reality, it's very fragile and unstable. And that's why they like to surround themselves with people who also have low self-esteem — but who deal with it in the opposite way by not making themselves bigger, but smaller than they are. And that's why they believe the myth that they can't do anything and are worth nothing.

Those who believe in themselves and know their abilities neither need to keep others down to feel better — nor to please everyone to beg for favor.

Does that make sense? Good. But how do you build healthy self-confidence?

What Can You Do Well?

Take a moment to grab a sheet of paper and a pen. Please don't just do this exercise in your head, because your subconscious won't recognize it as a search query.

And it's only if your subconscious understands that you want to learn something about yourself, and that this is so important to you that you plan to write it down, will you get the most out of this exercise.

Because then it will have a lasting effect, and you'll continue to come up with things afterward – which, of course, you should add to your list.

Since you've likely never done this exercise before, you might initially be convinced that you don't do many things well, don't possess many good qualities, and overall, consider yourself quite insignificant.

That's exactly why you need a written list, one you can return to in the coming weeks and months to supplement. It doesn't work in your head; the exercise would just dissipate uselessly.

Enough preamble, let's get started: First, write down all the things you're good at.

Don't just think about professional skills or talents, but also personal strengths, such as patience, empathy, or creativity.

If you can't think of anything, ask friends or family members. They often see things in us that we can't see ourselves.

Next, list your weaknesses. Be honest with yourself but also kind. Everyone has weaknesses, and recognizing them is the first step towards becoming the best version of yourself.

Remember, weaknesses aren't necessarily negative; they're simply areas where you can grow.

Once you've made your list, take some time to look at it. How do you feel about the different points? Proud? Surprised? Motivated? These emotions are important indicators of what truly matters to you and where your passions lie.

Now that you have a clear understanding of your strengths and weaknesses, set some goals.

Choose a strength you want to further develop and a weakness you want to work on.

Make a plan on how you can achieve both goals. Perhaps you'd like to read a book on the topic you want to improve on – like this book here…

You might want to attend a seminar or workshop – how about a rhetoric seminar to give your arguments more weight and to better assert yourself?

Or you might even want to find a coach or a mentor.

Remember to regularly review and update your list. Your strengths and weaknesses can change over time, and it's important that your list reflects your current situation.

This exercise is a lifelong process that helps you understand yourself better and advance your personal development.

Don't forget to praise yourself for every progress you make. Even the smallest improvement is a step in the right direction.

By celebrating your strengths and working on your weaknesses, you build self-confidence and move closer to your goals.

And as a bonus, with the newfound self-confidence, you'll find it easier to say "No" more often, and do so with ease.

5. "MORE EN-EMIES, MORE HONOR"

Don't fear polarization! Why? It sharpens your profile and attracts precisely those people who truly resonate with your ideas. This leads to deeper and more authentic relationships.

Take a deep breath...

… for this chapter is dedicated to polarization – the brave decision to consciously not try to please everyone and instead to hold and express clear, sometimes divisive, opinions. And yes, this can indeed be meaningful and desirable.

Imagine you're standing in a vast room full of people. Everyone is talking at once, and you want your voice to be heard. But if you only repeat what everyone else is saying, your voice will get lost in the crowd.

However, if you say something new, perhaps even unexpected, heads suddenly turn in your direction. Suddenly, for a moment, you have everyone's attention focused on you.

No question, that can be scary at first – but on closer inspection, it's actually a huge opportunity.

Because that's exactly what happens when you polarize. You separate the wheat from the chaff, the fans from the critics, the followers from the haters. And that is not only brave but also strategically wise.

When you clearly state your opinion, people also know clearly what you stand for. This makes you unmistakable as a brand, as a person, as a voice.

Those who stay with you and stand by you are not just spectators. They are fans, allies, like-minded individuals. These relationships are deeper and more valuable than fleeting acquaintances on the surface.

Moreover, nothing ensures visibility in the crowd better than polarization. In a sea of uniformity, contrast is king!

Polarization makes you visible, memorable, and often worth discussing.

Yes, you will gain many opponents. But you will gain just as many new fans and supporters.

But What About the Fear?

The fear of not being liked is as human as the need to breathe. But here's a small, subtle, yet enormously important secret: It's impossible to please everyone.

If you try, you end up as the proverbial chameleon that, in its constant adaptation, forgets its own original color and neither stands out from its surroundings nor is noticed at all.

Therefore, please see polarization not only as a risk but truly also as an opportunity. An opportunity to be authentic, to find your true target audience, and to send a deeper message.

Yes, you will have critics, but remember the old saying: "More enemies, more honor."

The greatest changes and the strongest movements throughout human history were not driven by the quiet and conformist but by those willing to swim against the current.

How to Deal with Criticism

But to not leave you out in the cold, here's a quick overview of how you can calmly handle criticism and even welcome it:

1. Filter Feedback: Learn to distinguish constructive criticism from mere noise. Not every negative feedback is an attack; sometimes, it's an invaluable treasure that can propel you forward significantly.

2. Show Your Edge: Stay true to your core principles, even if you adjust your approach. Your authenticity is your strongest weapon.

3. Humor as a Shield: A smile can be harder than armor steel. Humor not only helps to break the ice but also to put criticism into perspective and relativize it. This includes the ability to laugh at yourself. And that can be practiced!

4. Reflect Before Reacting: Take a moment to process the feedback before responding. This pause can help you approach the situation with a clearer mind and less emotion.

5. Seek Clarity: If the criticism is vague, ask for specific examples to understand better what the issue is. This shows your willingness to improve and helps avoid misunderstandings.

6. Thank the Critic: Acknowledging someone's feedback can disarm potential conflict and open the door for constructive dialogue. It doesn't mean you agree, but it shows respect for their perspective.

7. Use it as a Learning Opportunity: Criticism can be a powerful tool for personal and professional growth. Analyze it to find actionable insights.

8. Share Your Viewpoint: If you disagree with the criticism, calmly and clearly explain your perspective. A constructive exchange of views can lead to mutual respect and understanding.

9. Set Boundaries: It's essential to protect your mental health. If criticism becomes personal attacks, it's okay to set boundaries and disengage.

10. Seek Support: Sometimes, external input can provide a fresh perspective. Discuss the criticism with trusted friends or mentors who can offer their insights and support.

And remember: Polarization is not the end of the dialogue; you can make it the beginning of a deeper, more meaningful conversation.

For those who share your vision, it's an invitation to come closer – and for everyone else, it's a clear message that it's okay to go separate ways.

In a world of too much superficial adaptation, be the unexpected twist, the compelling story one simply can't put down.

Because at the end of the day, it's much more satisfying to be loved or hated for what you are than to be appreciated for what you're not.

6. THE INNER JUDGE

A fantastic exercise from parts therapy: counterbalance your inner critic, who acts as the prosecutor, with a brilliant inner lawyer who defends you. In the end, the inner judge decides.

Brief Introduction to Parts Therapy

Imagine within you there exists a colorful ensemble of different "parts" or "self-aspects," each with its own personality, desires, and fears. These parts interact with each other like characters in a play, with each part playing a role in your psychological ecosystem. Parts therapy gives us the tools to conduct this ensemble rather than be dominated by it.

Parts therapy is based on the premise that our self is composed of many different parts that collectively shape our experiences, reactions, and behaviors.

Some of these parts are conscious to us, while others operate in the shadows, shaped by past experiences, particularly from childhood and adolescence. These parts can come into conflict with each other, leading to internal tensions and external challenges.

Each part has a role that was originally aimed at protecting us or fulfilling a need. For instance, there's the Protector, the Critic, the Caregiver, or the Adventurer.

These parts develop in response to our life circumstances and strive to shield us from psychological pain or motivate us towards certain actions. It's like having an internal orchestra, but not all instruments always play in harmony.

The Goal is Harmonious Coexistence

A key aspect of parts therapy is the awareness and acceptance of all inner parts. By acknowledging that each part has value and originally acted for our well-being, we can start to develop a more harmonious internal interplay.

It's about understanding the perspective of each part, listening to it, and empathetically addressing its needs and fears.

Through working with the inner parts, we learn how to resolve conflicts between them and negotiate a type of internal peace treaty. This process not only promotes our mental health but also allows us to live more authentically and holistically.

And now for the twist: You can also apply the techniques of parts therapy to bring more fairness into the inner courtroom trial where you constantly find yourself on the dock.

The Inner Courtroom

We all know it, the inner critic that bombards us with self-doubt and negative thoughts. But what if we finally assign a brilliant inner lawyer to this nagging prosecutor to passionately defend us? Imagine a courtroom where the inner judge ultimately has the final say:

1. The Inner Prosecutor: He accuses you of everything under the sun: "You're not good enough," "You'll never manage it," "Others are much more successful than you." His evidence seems convincing, his arguments persistent. But before we consider the verdict final, let's finally let the defender speak.

2. The Brilliant Inner Lawyer: Now imagine your inner lawyer standing up, organizing his files, and beginning to defend you with a calm but determined voice. "My client has already overcome numerous challenges," he argues, "every experience, good or bad, has led to valuable lessons." He presents evidence of your strengths, your passions, your small and big successes. He reminds the courtroom of your humanity, your ability to grow and learn.

3. The Decisive Dialogue: Now comes the twist—conduct a dialogue between your inner prosecutor and your inner lawyer. Let them debate, but ensure your inner lawyer gains the upper hand. He might retort, for example: "Yes, there were failures, but each one led to important self-realization and improvement."

4. The Inner Judge Decides: At the end of the day, the inner judge sits wisely and dignified, weighs the arguments, listens, and finally decides. The trick is to train this judge to rule fairly and wisely. Insights from the defense by the inner lawyer can help correct the self-image and develop more self-compassion.

Exercises for the Inner Courtroom

Parts therapy offers a rich palette of exercises that can help you gain a deeper understanding and better control over your inner dialogues. How about trying the following exercises:

1. Inner Role Play: Take some time to go through the role play between prosecutor and lawyer quietly. Maybe even write it down to get a clear perspective.

2. Defense Speech Writing: Write a speech where your inner lawyer presents all your strengths and successes. Read this speech in moments of doubt.

3. The Fair Judge: Practice being a fair judge for yourself. When criticizing yourself, ask: "Is this really true? Are there proofs to the contrary?"

4. Prepare a Counterstatement: Take a situation where you criticized yourself and work out a counterstatement from your inner lawyer. List all the arguments against the criticism, and remember situations where you were successful or overcame a challenge. This exercise helps to lessen the impact of the inner critic.

5. Call to the Witness Stand: Imagine your inner lawyer calling witnesses to testify on your behalf. These "witnesses" can be real or imaginary persons, memories of successes, or even your strengths and talents. Think about what these witnesses would say to affirm your value and achievements.

6. Court Recess: If you notice the inner dialogue becoming particularly intense, take a court recess. Use this time for a breathing exercise, meditation, or a walk. The break helps calm the mind and allows a clearer, more objective view of the inner trial.

7. Visualize the Verdict: Imagine in detail how your inner judge delivers a benevolent verdict. Envision how this fair judgment brings freedom from self-criticism and an affirmation of your strengths and abilities. This positive visualization can strengthen your self-perception and self-esteem.

8. Plea for Self-Care: Let your inner lawyer make a plea for more self-care and self-love. Write down why it's important to treat yourself well and how self-care can improve your quality of life and well-being.

9. Revision Process: Allow yourself to reconsider past "verdicts" of your inner judge. There might be self-criticisms or beliefs that, upon closer examination, no longer hold up. This process helps correct outdated and unhealthy self-images.

These exercises assist you in developing a balanced relationship between self-criticism and self-support. They can teach you to constructively shape your inner dialogues.

7. THE ROTTEN APPLE

A single rotten apple spoils the whole barrel. There's only one solution: timely sorting out.

In an idyllic orchard...

...where apples hang so red and juicy on the trees that you can smell them from afar, lies a timeless wisdom. A wisdom that is significant not just for fruit growers but for each of us in daily life.

It's the lesson of the "rotten apple."

As we all know: It only takes one rotten apple to spoil a whole crate of fresh, crisp apples.

The rotten apple is more than just a piece of spoiled fruit. It's a symbol for anything in our lives that has a negative influence—be it habits, beliefs, relationships, or even a task that drains more energy than it gives.

These "rotten apples" have the power to undermine our endeavors, goals, and even our well-being.

As in the orchard, so in our personal and professional lives: Timely recognition and sorting out these negative influences are crucial.

It's not about immediately banishing everything difficult from our lives. Not at all! Rather, it's about recognizing what harms us in the long run and then feeling brave enough to say "No."

But how do we recognize a "rotten apple"?

Sometimes it reveals itself through physical symptoms: a constant feeling of exhaustion that accompanies us despite enough sleep, or an inexplicable loss of joy in certain activities.

Other times, it's an emotional signal, like persistent dissatisfaction or recurring negative thoughts about a particular situation or person.

Sorting out requires courage and often a dose of self-reflection. It starts with the simple question:

"Does this feel good?"

If the answer is a hesitant or clear "No," then it might be time to take a closer look at this "rotten apple."

Again, it's not about impulsively removing all negatives from life. It's about consciously deciding what serves our well-being.

Saying a healthy "No" is a skill we can learn and refine over time. It's an act of self-care that allows us to set and maintain our boundaries.

The first step is often the hardest, but with each decision we make for our own well-being, the next step becomes easier.

How Exactly Do You Do That?

Here are various techniques and exercises designed to help you identify your "rotten apples" and say "No" with confidence:

1. Energy Diary: Keep a diary for at least a week, noting which activities and interactions energize you and which drain you. Pay special attention to emerging patterns. This exercise helps you become more aware of the situations or people that represent "rotten apples" for you.

2. The Two-List Method: Create two lists. On one list, write down everything that is important to you and brings you joy. On the other list, note what regularly drains your energy or causes discomfort. Compare both lists and think about how you can integrate more of what you love into your life and what you can reduce or eliminate.

3. The Chairs Technique: Place two chairs facing each other. Sit on one chair and imagine the "rotten apple" (a person, a task, etc.) sits on the other. Conduct an imaginary conversation in which you say "No" clearly and firmly. This technique helps you prepare for real conversations and organize your thoughts and feelings.

4. The Three-Question Technique: Before deciding for or against something, ask yourself three questions: "Does it serve my well-being?", "Is it in line with my values?", and "Am I comfortable with it?". If you hesitate on any of these questions, it might be an indication that it's a "rotten apple."

5. Visualization Exercise: Take a moment to visualize yourself in a future without the "rotten apple." How do you feel? What has improved? This exercise can show you the positive impacts of your "No" and encourage you to take the necessary step.

6. Role-Playing: Practice saying "No" with a trusted friend or family member. Role-playing provides a safe environment to go through various scenarios and familiarize yourself with possible reactions from others. This builds self-confidence and makes it easier to stand your ground in real situations.

7. Boundary Clarity Exercise: Write down where your personal boundaries lie. What's important to you in relationships, at work, and in other areas of life? Knowing your boundaries makes it easier to communicate and defend them.

8. Priority Matrix: Create a priority matrix to evaluate tasks and requests. Divide it into four quadrants: urgent and important, important but not urgent, urgent but not important, and neither urgent nor important. This can help you identify what truly deserves your "Yes."

9. Self-Compassion Pause: Whenever you're about to say "Yes" out of obligation or fear, take a self-compassion pause. Remind yourself that it's okay to prioritize your well-being and that saying "No" can be an act of self-care.

By applying these techniques and exercises, you strengthen your ability to recognize "rotten apples" and say "No" with confidence.

Every step towards a conscious and healthy "No" is a step towards a more fulfilled life.

Remember, it's okay to make room for new things by letting go of what no longer serves us.

8. NEGOTIATING AT EYE LEVEL

Adults should negotiate their relationships on an equal footing. At least, that's how it should be. Sometimes, however, equality is only apparent, namely as long as Person B does everything Person A says. But is that still equality?

A request without the option to say no is not a request but a command.

Sometimes we ask for something, but actually, we don't give the other person a real choice. A genuine request means that a "No" as an answer is perfectly fine. But what happens when that's not the case?

It depends on how we were shaped in our first relationships — that is, in our friendships as children and teenagers.

If we learned that it's entirely okay to say "No" sometimes, and the adults around us modeled reciprocity and equality in their interactions, then we will adopt this standard as adults.

We say "No" naturally and can't even imagine that there are people who find this difficult.

But what if our first relationships and friendships and our observations of adults provided us with entirely different experiences?

A vivid case Example

Imagine two teenagers, Anna and Beate, are friends. Anna has a certain way of seeing things: She believes that true friendship means that Beate should always say "Yes" to her requests.

She argues that a "No" would mean Beate is prioritizing her own needs over the friend's, which in Anna's eyes would be selfish. And surely Beate doesn't want to be selfish?

No, of course, Beate doesn't want to be selfish! And she definitely doesn't want to risk losing Anna – so she dares not refuse a request.

After some years, Beate has adopted the wrong belief that true equality in a relationship means always saying yes.

That this only applies to Beate, and Anna quite often and happily says "No," doesn't even register with Beate – she's too busy trying to please Anna. She doesn't notice the lack of true equality in this friendship.

Years later, Dirk enters Anna's life. Dirk and Beate are on the same wavelength, and Dirk respects Beate and treats her as an equal.

Dirk asks Beate for something, and a "No" would be perfectly okay for him because Dirk assumes actual equality. But Beate, shaped by Anna's viewpoint, thinks she must always agree to maintain the friendship or relationship. Dirk, assuming real equality, has no idea about this.

Every time Dirk asks Beate for a favor, she says "Yes" – not because she wants to, but because she believes she has to.

Dirk takes the "Yes" at face value, thinking everything is fine, and so he keeps asking her for favors. He hasn't received any signals of boundaries – which he would, of course, respect immediately! And surely Beate could ask him for favors anytime too!

Beate, on the other hand, feels like Dirk is unreasonably demanding things she doesn't want to do and that she's just saying "Yes" to keep the peace.

Internally, she begins to resent feeling taken advantage of and exploited.

The gap between what's going on in her head and reality grows wider. Beate gets lost in her own narrative, and Dirk has no clue.

When Beate finally explodes and ends the friendship, Dirk is completely taken aback and doesn't understand what's happening.

Dirk is confused and hurt. He always believed his relationship with Beate was based on mutual respect and understanding. Suddenly, he's left with a puzzle whose pieces no longer fit together. He wonders where he went wrong, not realizing the problem runs deeper.

Beate, on the other hand, feels relieved and free, yet also guilty and sad. She's gathered the courage to say what she should have long ago, but now she's plagued by doubts about whether she acted correctly — especially when she sees Dirk's reaction, she wonders if she might have overreacted, and she misses Dirk deeply.

She feels her old fear of saying "No" is confirmed because she's now experienced that it destroyed the relationship when she finally did say "No."

But let's pave the way for a happy ending and have them attend just a few sessions of couples therapy — that's all they really need.

The therapist quickly recognizes the dynamic between them, as it's so common. A routine situation in couples therapy, so to speak.

During these discussions, the therapist gently opens both their eyes to the misunderstandings and unspoken expectations between them. Dirk hears for the first time about Beate's inner conflict and her fears of always having to comply to avoid disturbing the harmony. Beate, in turn, realizes that her inability to say "No" not only strained her relationship with Dirk but also heavily burdened her self-esteem.

The therapist carefully explains that true friendship and love must provide space for honesty, boundaries, and most importantly, the ability to say "No."

Beate understands she is responsible for leaving behind the old conditioning influenced by Anna, to improve her communication, and to set clear boundaries. Saying "Yes" when you mean "No" is a slow poison: for the relationship and for one's self-esteem.

Beate and Dirk decide to move forward with open and transparent communication, clearly articulating their needs and boundaries. Beate promises Dirk that in the future, when she says "Yes," it truly means "Yes." Dirk reiterates to Beate that she should feel free to ask him for favors too — and that she can trust that a "Yes" from him is genuine. More importantly, he assures her that a "No" is not a catastrophe.

This might all sound straightforward and logical, but Beate and Dirk are aware that the path to open communication and mutual understanding is paved with challenges.

There will be days when it's harder for Beate to say "No," and moments when doubts might overshadow their new insights.

However, they are determined to work on their relationship and support each other through this process.

They agree to have regular "check-in" conversations, where they openly discuss how they feel, what they need, and how they can continue to improve their communication. These discussions serve as a safe space where both can express their feelings without fear of judgment or consequences.

This story underscores the importance of honest communication and the mutual respect necessary for healthy relationships. By addressing their misunderstandings and committing to clear and open dialogue, Beate and Dirk not only salvage their relationship but also set a foundation for deeper connection and understanding.

It's a testament to the idea that acknowledging and respecting each other's boundaries strengthens bonds, rather than weakens them. Through their journey, they learn that true intimacy and partnership are built on the bedrock of authenticity, where both individuals feel seen, heard, and valued for who they truly are.

Let's go back to our starting point

If we were conditioned to believe that our worth is tied to our compliance, saying "No" might feel like an insurmountable challenge. We might fear rejection, conflict, or losing the relationship entirely if we don't meet the other person's expectations or demands.

In such cases, learning to negotiate relationships at eye level as adults requires unlearning these early patterns and establishing new norms for ourselves.

This involves recognizing our right to set boundaries, to express our needs and desires without fear, and to accept that healthy relationships allow for both parties to say "No" without repercussions.

Building this skill set is not just about personal growth; it's about creating healthier, more balanced relationships where all parties feel respected and valued. Here are some strategies to start this process:

1. Reflect on Your Beliefs: Consider the beliefs you have about saying "No" and where they come from. Challenge the idea that compliance is necessary for acceptance.

2. Practice Small: Start by saying "No" in low-stakes situations where the risk of conflict or loss feels minimal. This helps build confidence in your ability to assert your needs.

3. Communicate Openly: Practice open and honest communication about your needs, desires, and limits. Clarity can prevent misunderstandings and help establish mutual respect.

4. Seek Reciprocity: In your relationships, strive for a balance of give and take. Notice if you're always the one accommodating and start to ask for what you need too.

5. Set Boundaries: Learn to set and enforce healthy boundaries. Clearly define what is acceptable and what is not in your relationships, and be prepared to uphold these boundaries respectfully but firmly.

6. Seek Support: If changing deeply ingrained patterns of behavior feels overwhelming, consider seeking support from a therapist or counselor. They can provide guidance and tools to help you navigate this process.

7. Empathetic Listening: Engage in empathetic listening to understand the needs and perspectives of others. This builds a foundation for mutual respect and open communication.

8. Role Model Healthy Behavior: Be a role model for healthy boundary-setting and communication in your relationships. This not only benefits you but can also positively influence those around you.

9. Understand the Difference Between Assertiveness and Aggression: Educate yourself on the difference between being assertive and being aggressive. Assertiveness is about expressing your needs and boundaries respectfully, without infringing on the rights of others.

10. Normalize Boundary Setting: Make boundary setting a normal and expected part of all your relationships. This helps create an environment where everyone feels safe to express their needs.

11. Reaffirm Your Self-Worth: Remind yourself regularly that your worth is not contingent on your compliance or ability to please others. You are valuable and deserving of respect, regardless of whether you say "Yes" or "No."

12. Practice Self-Care: Prioritize self-care as a critical aspect of maintaining your well-being. When you take care of yourself, you're better equipped to engage in healthy relationships.

13. Reflect on Relationship Dynamics: Regularly take time to reflect on the dynamics of your relationships. Identify any patterns that may be unhealthy or imbalanced and consider ways to address them.

14. Learn to Tolerate Discomfort: Recognize that saying "No" might initially feel uncomfortable or cause anxiety. Understand that this discomfort is part of the growth process and will diminish over time as you become more accustomed to asserting yourself.

15. Celebrate Progress: Acknowledge and celebrate each step you take towards healthier relationship dynamics, no matter how small. Recognizing your progress can motivate you to continue on this path.

Remember, negotiating at eye level is not just about saying "No"; it's about fostering respect, understanding, and equality in your relationships.

9. SAFE AND UN-SAFE

There's a straightforward categorization you've probably never heard of—but it can greatly simplify the lives of people who always want to please everyone.

Knowing Who You Can Trust

Do you know people with whom everything just seems utterly simple? You don't have to think twice about how to act around them. They're uncomplicated, reliable, patient, and in their presence, you simply feel comfortable and well taken care of. Such people I call "safe."

And then there are the other kinds of people. With them, you feel like you have to handle them with kid gloves.

Inevitably, you walk on eggshells around them and treat them as if they're a raw egg, just to be on the safe side.

Their mood can turn on a dime if things don't go their way. They can become snappy, sarcastic, and offended from one moment to the next.

They're also quite moody and difficult to read. On a good day, they can be very charming and pleasant.

But you can never be quite sure when they might suddenly take offense— and their face clouds over as if a black cloud has passed in front of the sun.

Such people I call "unsafe." And unfortunately, you can't always avoid them completely—some family member, some colleague, perhaps even the boss might be "unsafe."

All you can do is try to make the best of it, limit contact to an absolute minimum, and not let it get you down too much. The only protection against such people, and the best way to endure them at all, is actually strong boundaries. But we'll talk about that in a separate chapter.

Here, however, we want to deal with another aspect of "safe" and "unsafe": why do people who want to please everyone and who find it hard to say "No" often have particularly many people around them who are "unsafe"?

Do You Attract People Who Are "Unsafe"?

Some people complain that they seem to always attract the same kind of people. "No matter what I do, I always end up with the wrong men!" a woman might complain to her best friend.

And on closer inspection, these men all fall under the "unsafe" category.

But does this woman really attract such men magically? The solution to the puzzle is actually much simpler.

Those who are "unsafe" can't change their stripes. And they find that most people avoid them. Of course, it's not their fault, because, in the minds of "unsafe" people, it's always the fault of others.

And thankfully, some people don't avoid them, although they could. Well, those people must have taste. And graciously, they're allowed to stay close and endure the whims of their Highness.

You see: You don't actually attract "unsafe" people. And they're not looking for you, specifically. You're simply among the few people who don't immediately run away and don't avoid the unpleasant companions.

So, you're literally the one who remains. That's the whole secret: "Unsafe" people are just scavengers!

Who's preventing the "unsafe" from learning? Well, you!

And now, please don't fall into pity for the poor unpleasant folks and don't consider yourself the Good Samaritan.

"But without me, they have no one!"

Exactly. Then, and only then, they would have to change. Or be alone and sulk bitterly, blaming the cruel world.

Often, they do this for a while—trying to guilt-trip others, as that always worked so well before, and often they're successful: The others return, guilt-ridden and repentant, and can now be even better controlled and manipulated due to their bad conscience.

Do you recognize yourself and your situation?

Only when no one engages in their foul play anymore and the "unsafe" people are left to their own devices is there suddenly a real motivation to, for a change, look at their own contributions to the situation, take themselves by the nose, and perhaps change a bit.

Surround Yourself with "Safe" People as Much as Possible

There's a wonderful saying: You can't change the people around you. But you can change the people around you.

Take a closer look at the people in your immediate circle. How many are "safe," and how many are "unsafe"? Can you improve the ratio? Are there "unsafe" individuals you can remove from your life?

For those you can't remove – for whatever reasons – (yet?), you could try to minimize contact and let the constant headwind of negative vibes bounce off you more easily.

Protective walls are indeed necessary for these people: as soon as you trust them and reveal a vulnerability, it will be used against you.

So, save that for people who are "safe" – and learn to distinguish both categories reliably from each other.

Building boundaries and cultivating positive connections

Here are some exercises to help you identify "safe" people in your environment and protect yourself from "unsafe" individuals:

1. Reflection Exercise: Take some time to think about each person in your immediate environment. Write down how you feel after interactions with each person. Do you feel energized and supported, or do you feel drained and diminished? This can help you distinguish between "safe" and "unsafe" individuals.

2. Boundary-Setting Practice: Identify one small boundary you can set with an "unsafe" person in your life. This could be as simple as saying "No" to a request that makes you uncomfortable or limiting the amount of time you spend with them. Practice setting this boundary in a safe environment, perhaps by role-playing with a trusted friend or family member.

3. Positive Affirmation List: Create a list of positive affirmations that reinforce your right to surround yourself with "safe" people. Examples might include "I deserve to be treated with respect," "My feelings and needs are valid," and "I have the right to choose who I spend my time with." Review and recite these affirmations regularly, especially when you're feeling doubtful about setting boundaries.

4. Gratitude Journal: Keep a gratitude journal where you specifically note the "safe" people in your life and the positive interactions or support they provide. This can help shift your focus towards the positive relationships in your life and reinforce your desire to cultivate more of these connections.

5. Visualization Exercise: Visualize a scenario where you successfully manage an interaction with an "unsafe" person by maintaining your boundaries and not allowing their behavior to affect your sense of self-worth. This can help build your confidence in handling challenging interactions.

6. Social Circle Audit: Make a list of your social circle, categorizing individuals as "safe" or "unsafe" based on your experiences with them. For the "unsafe" individuals, write down whether you can limit interaction or need to develop strategies to protect your well-being during necessary interactions.

7. Self-Care Plan: Develop a self-care plan for after you interact with "unsafe" individuals. This could include activities that help you recover and feel good about yourself, such as spending time in nature, practicing a hobby, or being with "safe" friends and family.

By regularly practicing these exercises, you can become more adept at recognizing "safe" versus "unsafe" people and protecting your well-being accordingly.

10. ASK INSTEAD OF MIND REA-DING

In anticipatory obedience, we often do what we believe others expect of us. But is that assumption correct?

The Tale of the Bread Roll Halves

Once upon a time, there was an old couple celebrating their 50th wedding anniversary with a wonderful breakfast.

For 50 years, it had been their ritual for the wife to slice the rolls and give her husband the top half. She loved him and wanted only the best for him.

So, for his sake, she gave up the delicious top half of the roll, which she herself enjoyed, and handed this delicacy to her husband.

And, of course, she couldn't reverse this gesture over time, as she didn't want her husband to think her love had diminished.

However, on their 50th anniversary, as she was slicing the rolls in the kitchen, she hesitated, and tears welled up in her eyes.

"For 50 years, I've given up the best half of the roll for my husband," she thought. "It's so unfair. Just for once, on our anniversary, I want to enjoy the top half of the roll. I hope my husband will understand and forgive me." With trembling hands, she brought the sliced rolls outside and, for the first time in their 50 years together, gave her husband the bottom halves.

The husband took one of the bottom halves, looked at it for a long time, and tears welled up in his eyes.

"My dearest," he finally said quietly, "I thank you. For 50 years, I've given up my favourite half of the roll for you, so you can have it, because I love you so much. And to-day, on our 50th anniversary, you're giving it to me. What a gift. I thank you."

Seeking Approval: Where Does It Come From?

The desire to be liked by others, to avoid conflicts with our closest relationships, is deeply rooted in human nature.

This is not surprising when considering how a small child is utterly dependent on the protection and care of their caregivers. A baby cannot survive alone – and it knows this instinctively. Instinctively and emphatically, it also knows how to express its needs, for its survival depends on these being met.

As the child grows older and its needs become more complex, it quickly learns to navigate the delicate balance between demanding its (no longer exclusively life-saving) needs and adapting to the needs of its caregivers. And in the hustle and bustle of everyday life, it's often signaled that its desires count less than those of adults.

The child may even get the impression that the parents' love is not unconditional but dependent on being "good." On putting its own wishes aside and conforming to the parents' desires. And that it's loved more – is more "lovable" – the more "easy-going" it is.

In the worst case, the child even tries to anticipate what its caregivers would like it to be. It develops ever finer antennas for recognizing how it should behave in the eyes of others to secure their love.

Because "love isn't free; you have to earn it," the child increasingly believes. And it begins to contort itself.

The question, "What do I actually want?" fades into the background.

For an adult who gained this impression as a child, it eventually becomes second nature. And they can't escape it.

Yet, even with a childhood full of love and security, we still harbor the instinctive desire for others to think well of us.

Because that means safety — whoever likes us, according to the unconscious calculation, probably won't attack us.

They might even help us, include us in their group, and our chances of survival increase (yes, our unconscious is very dramatic, as it has no sense of time, and our instincts still like to tell it about saber-toothed tigers and survival struggles).

On the other hand, if we're rejected, disliked, if we're outsiders — then we must leave the group, might even be attacked, and our chances of survival decrease.

Ask Instead of Mind Reading

But apart from the fact that it rarely comes down to our survival nowadays: We can't actually know what other people expect from us. We just assume. And if we sometimes knew what others REALLY think, or if we actually had the courage to just ask, we would be surprised how often we are also wrong.

Of course, no one can read minds, and believe me, you're definitely no exception!

So, get used to asking a few simple questions: "What do you mean by that?", "What do you think about this?", "I get the impression you're angry/sad/thoughtful/disappointed, is that right?" Or even just "Can you tell me a little more about it?"

Small, harmless questions that can change your life because then you're no longer basing your reactions on vague guesses and attempts at mind reading, but on facts. And that's always the better foundation.

And as a small but significant side effect, such questions also go down very well with your fellow humans. After all, by asking, you show interest in the other person, in their opinion, their feelings, making them feel heard and seen — and who doesn't like that?

And looking at it from the other side: Who likes it when their counterpart thinks: "I know exactly what's going on inside you, because I know you better than you know yourself!"?

That's presumptuous – and much less well-received than simply asking. So dare to ask!

Imagine asking questions like opening a window in a stuffy room. A room filled with the miasma of misunderstandings and assumptions, which stand like an invisible wall between people.

With every question you ask, you open this window a little further, letting in fresh air and sunlight. This simple act disperses the stuffy air of uncertainty and lets a clear, refreshing wind of clarity and understanding flow through the room. Suddenly, things look clearer, and what was once hidden becomes visible and understandable.

Like the sun dispelling darkness, your questions illuminate the shadows of doubt. They create an atmosphere where people not only feel seen and heard but also find the courage to open up and share.

And in this light of understanding, relationships grow and thrive, strong and vibrant like plants that have finally found the light.

11. CULTIVATING THE "SO WHAT?" ATTITUDE

Each of us has a clear idea of who we are and who we want to be. And that's how we want others to see us too. But what if they don't play along?

Our Self-Image Makes Us Vulnerable to Manipulation

Deep within our being, each of us carries an image of ourselves, an idea of who we are and who we wish to be. This self-image acts like an invisible compass, guiding us through the vast social ocean.

But what happens when the waves turn against us when the people around us fail to recognize or acknowledge our carefully curated image?

The human urge to be liked and acknowledged is deeply embedded in our psyche, stemming from our evolutionary past where belonging determined our survival.

But when others question our self-image, it can hit us even harder than this primal instinct to be liked at all costs.

We feel challenged in our very core and would do just about anything imaginable to convince the doubter of our self-image.

Why is this? Why does it affect us so deeply when someone questions how we see ourselves?

All a Matter of Identity

The strong reaction we experience when our self-image is doubted comes from the central importance of our identity to our entire being.

Our self-image is like an internal compass guiding us through life. It's a cocktail of our beliefs, values, experiences, and hopes that not only determines how we perceive the world around us but also how we move within it.

When this image is questioned by others, it feels as though our compass is suddenly malfunctioning, as if we are lost at sea without direction.

This sense of loss and uncertainty is deeply unsettling because it raises fundamental questions about ourselves and our place in the world.

It forces us to confront the possibility that our perception of ourselves—this carefully constructed self-understanding that we have nurtured over years—might not fully align with reality or others' perceptions.

This discrepancy between self-perception and how others see us confronts us with the fear of rejection and isolation, rooted deep in our evolutionary fears.

The intensity of our reaction to such challenges often relates to our need for what's called cognitive consistency—the desire to maintain a stable self-image.

Discrepancies between our self-image and how others perceive us create psychological tension that we find almost unbearable, and we attempt to resolve it, sometimes at any cost. This effort can lead us to defend or adapt ourselves in extreme ways, in an attempt to protect our self-image and maintain our social bonds—at all costs.

That's why our own self-image can make us emotionally vulnerable to the opinions and acknowledgment of others.

The Limits of Our Control

The harsh truth, however, is that we have no control over the thoughts and opinions of others. Period! We cannot peer into their minds, shape their views, or dictate their reactions.

If we nevertheless attempt to build our self-esteem on this shaky foundation, we're building a house on sand. The thoughts of other people are like the wind—constantly in motion and beyond our control.

It's time for you to stop attempting the impossible. Instead, focus on what's possible: gradually try out a new attitude—the "So What?" attitude.

The "So What?" attitude invites us to ask ourselves: "If someone doesn't like me or doesn't recognize my performance—so what? Does that really change my worth as a person?"

The answer is liberating, as it leads us to realize that our worth does not depend on external validation.

Are you familiar with the anecdote about the teacher who wanted to teach her students just that?

In an inspiring lesson, she demonstrated a powerful lesson about self-worth to her students. She started the lesson with a pristine banknote in her hand—fresh, untouched, and of recognizable value. "How much is this banknote worth?" she asked, holding up the note so everyone could see. The response was immediate and unanimous: "20 Euros!"

Then, in front of everyone, the teacher crumpled the banknote, threw it on the ground, and stepped on it with her shoes.

She picked it up again, now crumpled and dirty, its corners bent, its luster lost. "And now?" she asked again, "How much is it worth now?"

Despite its battered appearance, the students still confidently exclaimed: "Still 20 Euros!"

The teacher smiled. "Exactly," she said. "No matter how much I crumple it or step on it, its value remains unchanged. You are like this banknote. No matter how much others may criticize, judge, or try to pull you down—your value remains. You must never forget that your worth does not depend on the opinions or treatments of other people."

This simple, yet powerful demonstration left an indelible impression on the students. They learned that their self-worth is intrinsic, arising independently of external influences—a lesson in self-respect and resilience that would accompany them throughout their lives.

Practical Steps Towards the "So What?" Attitude

1. Self-Reflection: Take time to explore your self-image. What truly defines you? Is it the likes on social media, or your deep, personal successes and values that maybe only two or three close friends know about?

2. Recognition of Your Own Values: Identify what is genuinely important to you. What are your core values and strengths? Recognizing what lies within you forms a solid foundation for your self-esteem.

3. Acceptance of Uncontrollability: In moments of insecurity, remind yourself that the opinions of others are beyond your control. Practice the art of letting go.

4. Identify Triggers: Keep a journal for a week and note down moments when you feel your self-worth is being questioned or when you find yourself seeking external validation. Identifying these triggers can help you understand patterns and prepare you to apply the "So What?" attitude more effectively.

5. Set Achievable Personal Goals: Create personal goals that are aligned with your values and not influenced by others' expectations or opinions. Achieving these goals will reinforce your sense of self-worth and independence.

6. Meditation and Mindfulness: Incorporate meditation or mindfulness practices into your daily routine. These practices can help you stay centered and maintain a calm perspective when facing situations that might challenge your self-image. They reinforce the understanding that your worth is not contingent on external approval.

7. Positive Self-Talk: When you notice you're becoming dependent on others' opinions, pause and change the tone of your inner voice. Replace self-criticism with self-support and recognition.

8. Embrace the "So What?" Attitude: Imagine specific situations where you've felt rejected or misunderstood before, and respond with an internal "So what?". Practice making this attitude your emotional shield.

By adopting the "So What?" attitude, we not only navigate life's challenges with greater ease but also open ourselves up to a more authentic, self-determined life. It's the path to true freedom—the freedom to be ourselves, independent of the opinions and judgments of others.

Remember the lesson of the teacher with the banknote (such powerful demonstrations are known as impact techniques).

No matter how many people tread on you, your value remains unaffected.

And with this knowledge, it should already be much easier for you to confidently and with stable self-worth leave such a situation.

12. JOURNEY INTO THE PAST

"Everyone has their burdens," as the saying goes. We all carry a backpack from the past with us, filled with many useful items but also some unnecessary baggage. It's worthwhile to check if there's anything you can sort out. Doing so can make life lighter.

What Does Your Backpack Look Like?

Imagine your life as a journey. Your backpack, initially packed by your parents, contains everything they found important and helpful on their own life's journey. Naturally, they wanted to pass these things on to their child for their journey, so they packed them into the backpack.

There are likely many useful things in it, but also probably some baggage that just takes up space in your backpack on your personal life path, unnecessarily costing you energy and therefore should be sorted out.

Take this opportunity to check your backpack. How heavy is this backpack? Are you carrying things you no longer need? Or is the most important thing missing because others packed it, who of course couldn't have known your future path?

Maybe you'll find beliefs and expectations in your backpack that are more of a burden than support. Maybe you'll also discover skills and dreams that were buried deep because someone thought they weren't so important to you.

Or you might come across old wounds and fears that weigh on your back like stones, making your steps heavier than they need to be.

Each item in your backpack tells a story - stories about where you come from and who you are, but not necessarily where you're going or who you could be.

It's Time to Thoughtfully Repack Your Backpack

Start by taking each item in hand and asking yourself: Does it serve my path? Does it support the goal of my journey?

It can be painful to part with some things because they're familiar and safe, even if they're heavy. But remember, every burden you drop makes your step a little lighter and makes room for new things.

Remember to pack new things in your backpack too. Perhaps they are new skills you want to learn, or positive beliefs that give you strength.

Maybe they are just memories you collect as you move forward, shining moments of joy and satisfaction that no one can take away from you.

These new items are your personal treasures, selected and collected by you, for your path.

And don't forget: Your backpack is dynamic, just like your life. What is important today may be unnecessary tomorrow.

So be ready to re-evaluate, repack, and make room for change again and again. This way, your backpack won't become a burden that weighs you down but a treasure chest full of tools, memories, and dreams that accompanies and enriches you on your life's journey.

Your life is a journey, and you are the only one who can decide what you want to take with you. Make your backpack a symbol of freedom and self-determination, not burden and compulsion. In this way, every new experience, every step on your path, becomes not just lighter but also more meaningful and fulfilling.

Backpack Packing Guide

Here are some exercises that can help you check and repack your metaphorical backpack:

1. Backpack Inventory: Find a quiet corner with a sheet of paper and a pen. Imagine unpacking your backpack. List everything you "take out": beliefs, values, expectations, hopes, fears, dreams, etc. Examine each item and ask yourself: Does this help me on my path? Is it a burden or a support?

2. Letter to Your Younger Self: Write a letter to your younger self with advice on which "items" to pack in the backpack. This helps you reflect on which resources and insights you have valued over your life, promoting a deeper understanding of your personal development and values.

3. The Ballast Drop: Choose an "item" (a belief, a fear, an expectation) that you feel holds you back. Write down on a piece of paper why and how this item has become a burden. Then, tear the paper as a symbolic gesture of shedding this weight, and consider what you would like to pack in your backpack instead.

4. The Treasure Map: Create a treasure map for your life. Draw paths, obstacles, and treasures you want to discover. Consider which "equipment items" you need for this journey. This exercise helps you focus on your goals and consider what resources (new skills, knowledge, relationships) you need to collect to realize your dreams.

5. The Backpack Repack Plan: After deciding which items to keep, discard, or add, create a plan for how to repack your backpack. Set goals for the next week, month, and year. How will you acquire or develop these new items? How will you ensure your backpack stays light so you can enjoy your journey?"

6. Visualization of Future Self: Sit in a quiet place, close your eyes, and visualize your future self, say 5, 10, or 20 years from now. What "items" does this future self have in their backpack? What have they discarded? This exercise helps you align your current packing choices with the person you aspire to be.

7. The Gratitude List: Make a list of things in your backpack (metaphorically speaking) for which you're grateful.

This could include experiences, lessons learned, or personal strengths. Recognizing what enriches your journey can help you prioritize what to keep and what new treasures to seek.

8. Consultation with Trusted Guides: Have a conversation with trusted friends, family members, or mentors about what they see as your most valuable "items." Sometimes, others can offer perspective on the strengths and resources you may overlook or undervalue in yourself.

9. The "Why" Deep Dive: For each item you decide to keep in your backpack, write down why it's important to you. This exercise helps to reinforce the value of these items and ensures that what you carry truly aligns with your personal values and journey.

10. Crafting Your Personal Mantra: Based on your insights from these exercises, create a personal mantra or affirmation that encapsulates your philosophy for what you choose to carry in your life's backpack. This mantra can serve as a reminder to maintain a purposeful and light load as you move forward.

By engaging with these exercises, you're not just sorting through physical or metaphorical possessions; you're curating a life aligned with your deepest values, aspirations, and joys. Remember, the journey of life is ongoing, and what you carry can evolve just as you do.

13. SELF-CARE IS NOT A LUXURY

You can only give what you have—therefore, self-care is absolutely not selfish. Especially if you like to give to others, it is not only your right but practically your duty to ensure that you can always draw from a full well.

Balance between Giving and Taking

The idea of taking time for oneself seems like pure luxury to some people, something that can only be afforded once all other "more important" tasks are completed. Yet, the truth is that self-care is not optional but essential for our mental health, as without it, we quickly risk burning out.

Self-care means giving yourself permission not to always put your own needs last. However, it also doesn't mean that you should always put your needs ahead of others from now on.

It simply means that you are allowed to place your own needs alongside those of others, so that giving and taking are balanced in the long run.

This is a law of nature: You can only give what you have. And this applies to physical, mental, and emotional energy as well.

The paradox of self-care is that it's often difficult precisely because it's so necessary. In the moment we need it the most, it seems the least urgent.

Herein lies the challenge: Self-care must be a conscious decision, a firm commitment to oneself that is as important as any other responsibility in our lives.

Because self-care is not an act of selfishness but an act of self-love and self-respect. It allows us to act from a position of strength rather than exhaustion. It teaches us to set boundaries, to say "No" when necessary, and "Yes" to what nourishes and fulfills us. It's the acknowledgment that to be there for others, we first need to take care of ourselves.

In an era where burnout and stress are omnipresent, the message is clear: Self-care is not a luxury but a non-negotiable necessity.

It's truly high time to move self-care from the optional "Nice-to-have" list to the "Must-have" category. Because, at the end of the day, how we treat ourselves is not only a reflection of our self-esteem but also a model for how we shape and influence the world around us.

Here are some exercises to translate the concept of self-care into practical actions and help make it an integral part of your life.

Exercises for Enhanced Self-Care

1. Self-Care Plan: Take the time to create a weekly self-care plan. Choose a small self-care activity for each day of the week that brings you joy or peace. This could range from a 10-minute walk, reading a chapter in a book, to a short meditation. The key is to anchor these activities as fixed appointments in your calendar, just as you would with work meetings.

2. Self-Care Alarm: Set a daily alarm on your phone as a reminder to take a conscious break for self-care. Use this time to breathe consciously, enjoy a moment of silence, or simply drink a cup of tea. The alarm serves as a reminder that taking time for yourself is important, even if it's just for a few minutes.

3. Practice Saying "No": Saying "no" without feeling guilty is a matter of practice. Start with small things and gradually work your way up. The goal is to set boundaries and preserve your time and energy for activities that are good for you. This can be challenging but is an essential step to prevent overload and burnout.

4. The Self-Care Box: Create a self-care box with items that bring you joy or comfort. This could range from a favorite scent, a soft cloth, to an inspiring book. Turn to this box when you're feeling stressed or need a pick-me-up.

5. Schedule Nature Time: Make it a point to spend regular time in nature. Whether it's a walk in the park, gardening, or simply sitting on a bench observing your surroundings, time spent in greenery can do wonders for your mental and physical well-being.

6. Self-Care Rituals: Develop daily or weekly rituals where you dedicate yourself solely to self-care. This could be an evening bath, a weekly yoga session, or a Sunday brunch on your own. Choose activities that personally provide you with a sense of calm, joy, and rejuvenation.

7. Prioritize Physical Health: Pay attention to getting enough exercise, eating healthily, and getting plenty of sleep. Your body is the vehicle on your life's journey—treat it with respect and care.

8. Journey into the Past: To learn how to effectively care for yourself, it sometimes helps to take a journey into the past. Ask yourself: When did I start putting others' needs before my own? Were there moments in my life when I learned the wrong lesson that my needs are secondary? This journey can be painful, but it's necessary to recognize and break patterns. Only by understanding where these patterns come from can you begin to change them.

9. Mindfulness Meditation: Dedicate a few minutes each day to mindfulness meditation. Focus on your breath and observe your thoughts without judgment. This practice can reduce stress and increase self-awareness, making it easier to recognize when you need self-care.

10. Digital Detox: Set aside specific times for a digital detox. During this period, avoid using electronic devices. This break from digital stimuli can help reduce stress and improve sleep, allowing you to reconnect with yourself and your environment.

11. Creative Outlet: Find a creative outlet that resonates with you, such as painting, writing, cooking, or playing a musical instrument. Engaging in creative activities can be therapeutic and a powerful form of self-expression and self-care.

12. Self-Compassion Breaks: Whenever you notice you're being hard on yourself, take a self-compassion break. Speak to yourself with kindness, acknowledging your feelings and reminding yourself that imperfection is part of the human experience. Practicing self-compassion can significantly enhance your emotional well-being.

These exercises are designed to help make self-care a non-negotiable priority in your life and to show you how to treat yourself with the same kindness and care you extend to others. Self-care is not selfish; it's necessary. By caring for yourself, you fill your own cup so that you are also able to be there for others without losing yourself. One can only give what one has!

14. LEARNING TO VISUALIZE

Visualization exercises can be an incredibly powerful tool if you want to develop the ability to say "No" kindly but confidently. Think you lack the imagination for it? It's worth a try!

The Power of Mental Images

Visualization exercises are an immensely effective technique used in various disciplines—from elite sports to psychotherapy—to enhance performance, overcome fears, and learn new skills. By deliberately imagining certain situations and the associated positive feelings, we prepare our brain and body to implement them in reality.

The principle behind visualization is simple, but its impact is profound. By mentally rehearsing a situation where you say "No" clearly and firmly, you're training not just your mind to get used to this action, but also your body to respond calmly and confidently.

This mental practice creates a kind of blueprint in your consciousness that you can then call upon in real situations.

It's like training a muscle: the more you use it, the stronger and more reliable it becomes.

Step-by-Step Guide

To fully unlock the potential of visualization, start with the following steps:

1. Find a Quiet Place: Choose a location where you can be undisturbed and relax. A calm environment helps your mind focus and enter the deep concentration state necessary for effective visualization.

2. Relax Your Body: Use a simple yet effective breathing exercise. Sit or lie down comfortably and close your eyes to focus entirely on your breath. Breathe slowly and deeply through your nose, counting to four. Hold your breath for a moment, count to four again, then slowly exhale through your mouth, counting to six. Repeat this cycle three to five times. With each exhalation, release physical tension and signal your body that you wish to enter a state of deep relaxation.

3. Getting Serious: Imagine a situation where you typically find it hard to say "No". Start with a relatively low difficulty level, a situation where not much depends on a "No". You can increase the difficulty level with each exercise performance.

4. Use All Senses: The more vividly you can imagine the situation, the more effective the exercise. What do you see, hear, feel, smell, or even taste in this situation? Including all senses makes the experience more real and the learning effects stronger. Every hypnotherapist utilizes this principle in their hypnoses, trying to engage all your senses - do the same, as it significantly amplifies the effect!

5. Focus on the "No": Now imagine saying "No" clearly and distinctly. Pay attention to how you say it, what posture you adopt, how your voice sounds, and what facial expression you have. Make this "No" as realistic as possible in your mind.

6. Feel the Consequences: Visualize the immediate consequences of your "No". How do other people react? Importantly, imagine yourself accepting their reactions without feeling bad.

7. Identify Your Feelings: Pay attention to how you feel after saying "No". You might feel a mix of relief and fear, but focus on the feeling of strength and self-respect that comes with your decision.

8. Reflect and Adjust: After each visualization exercise, take a moment to reflect on the experience. What worked well? What could you improve next time? This reflection allows you to refine your visualization technique and make it even more effective.

9. Positive Reinforcement: After each visualization where you successfully say "No", visualize rewarding yourself. It could be something as simple as a mental pat on the back, a favorite treat, or some quality time doing something you love. This positive reinforcement strengthens the connection between assertiveness and personal gratification.

10. Visualization of Alternatives: In situations where saying "No" might be difficult, visualize yourself offering alternatives. This not only prepares you to maintain your boundaries but also to navigate social interactions more fluidly, showcasing your problem-solving and empathetic skills.

11. Peer Support Visualization: Imagine a supportive friend or mentor is with you during challenging situations. Visualize their encouraging words or presence bolstering your confidence to say "No". This exercise can help reinforce the feeling that you're not alone in your journey towards assertiveness.

12. Future Reflection: Visualize looking back from the future at moments you said "No". Imagine the long-term benefits and positive changes that came from these decisions. This perspective can help reinforce the importance of setting boundaries for your future well-being.

13. Repeat the Exercise Regularly: As with physical training, regularity is key to success in mental training. Dedicate a few minutes to this practice daily to achieve the best results—yes, you have the time, whether it's during your time on the "quiet throne," the morning shower, or the minutes before falling asleep. The more often you perform this visualization, the more familiar and confident you will feel about saying "No" in reality.

The Power of Positive Reinforcement

In addition to directly preparing for specific situations, visualization also contributes to strengthening your self-confidence and self-esteem more generally. When you regularly see yourself in positive scenarios where you successfully set boundaries and say "No," you also reinforce the image of yourself as a strong, confident individual. This positive self-perception is a powerful ally in many aspects of life, not just when it comes to saying "No."

Visualization exercises can thus be a key element on your path to greater self-confidence and autonomy. They allow you to develop exactly the skills in a completely safe, controlled environment—your imagination—that will then support and strengthen you in real life.

15. PERFECTION IS THE WOLF IN SHEEP'S CLOTHING

On your journey to learn how to say "No," perfectionism is not your friend but a hidden enemy. The fear of not being perfect often prevents us from setting boundaries and standing up for our own needs.

Where Does the Desire to Be Perfect Come From?

Perfectionism is deeply rooted in the desire for recognition and the fear of rejection. Many of us have learned that success and love are conditional: contingent upon being perfect. However, this constant pursuit of perfection is a race without a finish line, leaving us exhausted and dissatisfied over time. Because when is good truly good enough? Perfectionism says: never!

The consequences range from constant stress and overworking to deep dissatisfaction with oneself. Our perfectionism can prevent us from taking on new challenges, for fear of failing or not meeting high expectations. In the context of saying "No," perfectionism leads us to overextend ourselves in the long run because we believe we have to manage everything to be seen as perfect. We think that's the only way we've earned recognition and respect. And with that, we've fallen into the trap of perfectionism.

Overcoming Perfectionism—Here's How

Here are some exercises that can help you let go of the need for perfection:

1. Stop Viewing Perfectionism as a Friend: The first step to overcoming perfectionism is recognizing it as not a sign of strength, but a huge obstacle. Perfectionism only offers pseudo-security since it can never be achieved. Thus, good is never good enough, and your task can never be completed. Acknowledge that mistakes are human and completely normal—so you can take responsibility for your tasks and complete them, instead of eternally tweaking them.

2. Set Realistic Goals: Learn to set realistic goals that are actually achievable and celebrate the small successes along the way. This helps reduce pressure and find joy in the process itself, instead of chasing an unreachable perfect goal and feeling bad and inadequate.

3. Befriend Imperfection: Start to accept imperfection as part of human existence. Not everything has to be perfect, and often it's the small flaws that make life and work authentic and valuable.

4. Keep a Friendly-to-Errors Diary: Start a diary where you note down small "mistakes" or "imperfections" that happened to you each day, and reflect on how they did not have a negative impact on your life or even brought out positive aspects.

5. Apply the 80/20 Rule: For each task, consider which 20% effort provides 80% of the results. Focus on this 20% and give yourself permission not to perfect everything to 100%.

6. Practice Saying "No": Start in small, safe steps to say "No." Practice rejecting tasks or requests when you know accepting them would trigger your perfectionism. Start with situations where not much is at stake, and gradually work your way up. Every "No" strengthens self-confidence and the ability to stand up for oneself in more important matters.

7. Create a "Good Enough" List: Write a list of things where "good enough" is absolutely sufficient. This helps set priorities and recognize where perfectionism is unnecessary.

8. Intentionally Design Unperfect Leisure Time: Plan leisure activities where performance or results are not the focus. Hobbies where the process and not the perfect end result is the focus are ideal.

9. Imperfections Party: Host a small party or gathering where each participant shares a small imperfection or mistake. This promotes acceptance and shows that everyone has imperfections.

10. Seek Feedback: Ask friends, family, or colleagues for feedback on your work or behavior. Often, we find that our own standards are much higher than the expectations of others.

11. Celebrate Successes: Take time to celebrate your successes, even if they're not perfect. Acknowledge the value of your work and reward yourself for your effort, not just the outcome.

12. Gratitude Journal: Keep a journal where you write down three things you're grateful for each day. This can help you focus on the positive aspects of your life and reduce the pressure to be perfect.

13. Perfection Break: Intentionally set aside times when perfectionism is not allowed. This could be a creative break where you engage in activities just for the fun of it, without worrying about the outcome. For example, paint, draw, or write without judging the quality of your work.

14. The Comparison Ban: Challenge yourself to go a week without comparing yourself to others. Whether on social media, at work, or in personal life, remind yourself that your journey is unique and that comparison only fuels perfectionism.

15. Mindfulness Practice: Incorporate mindfulness exercises into your daily routine. Mindfulness can help you stay present and appreciate the current moment without obsessing over future outcomes or mistakes.

16. The Permission Slip: Write yourself a permission slip to make mistakes. Keep it in your wallet or post it somewhere visible as a constant reminder that it's okay to be imperfect.

17. Reframe Your Thoughts: Practice reframing your thoughts from negative to positive. For example, if you think "I must do this perfectly," change it to "I will do this to the best of my ability."

These exercises help you gradually calm your inner perfectionist and find more satisfaction and balance in your life. Remember, it's not about completely eliminating perfectionism but finding a healthy balance where you can appreciate yourself and your achievements without being burdened by unrealistic expectations.

16. COUNT YOUR BLESSINGS

There's a solid reason why so many psychotherapists recommend keeping a gratitude journal. The positive effects, both in the medium and long term, are simply astonishing.

The Science of Gratitude

Numerous studies consistently show that keeping a gratitude journal has several positive "side effects," including improved sleep quality, fewer symptoms of physical discomfort, increased resilience, and even an enhanced capacity for joy.

These benefits are partly due to gratitude's ability to focus attention on the present, stopping the mental hamster wheel that constantly worries about the future or ruminates over the past. Additionally, gratitude promotes positive emotions like joy, love, and enthusiasm, which directly contribute to reducing stress and anxiety.

Thus, maintaining a gratitude journal is much more than a pleasant pre-sleep routine. It's a powerful tool for changing life perspective and strengthening mental health. It's a method that helps alter the lens through which we view the world.

By regularly pausing to jot down what we're thankful for, we train our mind to recognize and appreciate the positive aspects of our lives, even amidst challenges and adversities.

This practice helps break the brain's often automatic tendency to focus on negative aspects.

This shift in perspective is enormously powerful, not only improving our mood instantly but potentially leading to deeper life satisfaction over time.

Over time, you can deepen your practice by not just noting what you're grateful for but also exploring why.

This additional level of reflection further enhances the feeling of gratitude by sharpening awareness of how exactly these things enrich your life.

How to Keep a Gratitude Journal

You might be thinking, "That's all well and good, but how do I start, and what should I pay attention to?" Here are some tips:

1. Make it a routine: Find a specific time each day to spend a few minutes writing in your gratitude journal. Many people find that the evening before bed is a good time to reflect on the day and practice gratitude.

2. Be specific: Instead of writing down general things you are grateful for, try to be specific. Write, for example, not just "for my friends" but "for the long phone call with my best friend today that gave me strength."

3. Look for the little things: Gratitude does not always have to relate to big events or life changes. Often, it's the small things that, when recognized, deepen our sense of gratitude. It could be the warm sunshine on your skin, a delicious meal, or a smile from a stranger.

4. Integrate photos: Make your gratitude journal more vivid by adding photos, small notes, or other memorabilia associated with the moments you are grateful for. These visual and physical reminders can enhance the positive feelings and help you remember the moments of gratitude more vividly.

5. Share your gratitude: Consider occasionally sharing entries from your journal with friends or family members. This can not only strengthen your relationships but also inspire others to begin their own practice of gratitude. Plus, sharing can add an extra layer of reflection and appreciation for the shared moments and relationships.

6. Expand your perspective: Try to find reasons for gratitude even in challenges or difficult situations. This exercise can be particularly powerful for building resilience and maintaining a positive attitude, even when life doesn't go as planned. Ask yourself: "What can I learn from this situation? Are there aspects I can still be thankful for?"

7. Combine your journal with meditation: Integrate your gratitude journal into your meditation practice by writing before or after meditating. This can help calm your mind and open you up to the practice of gratitude. Combining meditation and gratitude can amplify the effects of both practices.

8. Use self-created question catalogs: If you're having trouble getting started or don't know what to be grateful for on some days, use self-created question catalogs. Questions like "What am I grateful to my younger self for?", "Which person in my life made a difference today?", or "Which convenience do I often take for granted?" can help kickstart the writing process.

9. Be patient with yourself: Don't expect your life to change overnight, and be patient with yourself if you encounter days when gratitude is hard to feel. The practice of gratitude is a process that requires time and consistency. Each entry is a step towards deeper appreciation of your life and experiences.

10. Regularly look back: Take time now and then to read and reflect on your entries. This can help you recognize patterns – maybe there are specific people or activities that regularly appear and increase your happiness. This insight can give you valuable clues on how to make your life even more fulfilling.

11. Embrace Imperfection in Gratitude: Acknowledge that not every day will be filled with monumental achievements or moments. Some days, finding something to be grateful for might be as simple as appreciating a quiet moment to yourself or the absence of discomfort. Recognizing and valuing these seemingly mundane aspects can deepen your sense of gratitude and contentment.

12. Create a Gratitude Jar: Alongside your journal, keep a gratitude jar where you can drop in notes of gratitude daily. This visual representation of your grateful moments can be incredibly uplifting, especially when you physically see the jar filling up over time. On tougher days, reach into the jar and read a few notes to remind yourself of the good in your life.

13. Practice Gratitude with Others: Make it a point to express gratitude towards the people in your life. This could be through a simple thank you message, a compliment, or an act of kindness. Sharing gratitude not only strengthens your relationships but also multiplies the positive feelings associated with it.

14. Gratitude Reflection: At the end of each week, take a moment to review your gratitude journal entries. Reflect on the recurring themes or surprises. This weekly reflection can provide insights into what truly brings you joy and satisfaction, helping you focus more on these aspects in your life.

15. Gratitude and Goal Setting: Incorporate your gratitude practice into your goal-setting process. Before setting new goals, reflect on the past achievements and experiences you're grateful for. This can set a positive foundation for your aspirations and remind you of your strengths and accomplishments.

16. Challenge Negative Thoughts with Gratitude: Whenever you catch yourself dwelling on negative thoughts or worries, challenge them by thinking of three things you're grateful for. This practice can help shift your mindset and reduce the impact of stress and negativity.

17. Volunteer or Give Back: Engaging in volunteer work or finding ways to give back to your community can enhance feelings of gratitude. Seeing the impact of your contributions on others' lives can be a powerful reminder of the good in the world and the good within you.

18. Incorporate Gratitude into Daily Affirmations: Start your day with affirmations that include expressions of gratitude. Affirming positive thoughts about yourself and your life can set a grateful and optimistic tone for the day ahead.

19. Use Technology Wisely: Leverage apps or digital platforms that encourage gratitude practices. Whether it's a daily gratitude prompt via an app or participating in online gratitude challenges, technology can be a supportive tool in maintaining your practice.

20. Learn from Children: Spend time with children and observe their capacity for joy and gratitude in simple things. Their unfiltered appreciation for life can inspire a more genuine and heartfelt approach to your own gratitude practice.

By practicing and recording gratitude, you allow yourself to recognize beauty and joy in your life, even in difficult times. This practice can sustainably change your worldview from one of scarcity to one of abundance. You learn not to take the good in your life for granted but to celebrate and cherish it.

17. DO YOU TALK KINDLY TO YOURSELF?

Imagine talking to yourself in a way that uplifts and supports, especially after setbacks or failures. Some people speak to themselves so harshly that, if they spoke to their friends in the same manner, they'd likely have none left.

Is your inner dialogue destructive or constructive?

Maria is facing a crucial presentation at work, for which she has diligently prepared for weeks. Despite her efforts and preparations, things go awry on the presentation day. The technology fails, some of her key arguments are challenged, and she fumbles her words.

Leaving the meeting deeply disappointed, Maria immediately starts berating herself: "How could I, such an idiot, fail so miserably? I'm just not good enough for this job. I always mess everything up. I'm a failure, screwed up again. I can kiss my promotion goodbye. I'd be lucky if I don't get fired for being so dim-witted."

She dwells on this for hours, maybe even days, and each time she thinks about it, she repeats these negative self-talks, further undermining her self-esteem.

The way Maria talks to herself is a classic example of destructive self-talk. It's as if she has an inner critic that shows no mercy, harshly punishing her for every mistake and keeping her in a state of self-doubt and worthlessness. This kind of self-talk not only amplifies her negative feelings but can also lead to anxiety, depression, and low self-esteem over time.

Now, imagine Maria decides to change her internal dialogue. After the failed presentation, she begins to talk to herself as she would to a good friend in a similar situation: "It's okay that not everything went as planned today. I did my best, and that's what matters most. Everyone makes mistakes, and this was simply a learning opportunity, not evidence of my incompetence. Let's take a close look: What can I learn from this experience to do better next time?"

By consciously choosing a kinder and more supportive way to talk to herself, Maria begins to change her perspective. She realizes that failures and mistakes are part of the learning process and don't define her entire identity or capabilities.

This type of positive self-talk fosters resilience, self-compassion, and a healthier self-esteem. Maria learns to treat herself with the same kindness, understanding, and support that she would offer a good friend.

Sending Your Inner Critic to Leadership Training

Replacing destructive self-talk with kind, appreciative, and constructive self-dialogue is a powerful tool for personal development. But how do you do it? How can you send your inner critic to leadership training to learn to motivate rather than undermine self-esteem? The following steps can be helpful in initiating this process and transforming your inner critic into a benevolent mentor:

1. Identify and Name: The first step is to recognize the inner critic and give it a name. This helps create a conscious distance, realizing that this critical voice is not your entire personality but just a part of you. By naming your inner critic, you can more easily address and "instruct" it.

2. Initiate Dialogue: Start a dialogue with your inner critic. Ask about its intentions and what it's trying to protect. Often, the inner critic stems from a desire to shield us from shame, rejection, or failure. Understanding these intentions allows you to start changing its focus. Thank it for its efforts but also explain that its methods are unhelpful and often counterproductive.

3. Begin Retraining: Teach your inner critic new ways to express its positive intent without belittling you. Encourage it to provide constructive feedback focused on growth and learning rather than criticism and degradation.

4. Apply Specific Techniques: Use leadership coaching techniques, such as the sandwich method (positive statement – constructive criticism – positive statement) for self-talk. Start with acknowledging what went well, address what could be improved, and conclude with a motivating or hopeful outlook. Persuade your inner critic to adopt such techniques going forward.

5. Celebrate Successes: Pay attention to and celebrate progress. When your inner critic begins to communicate more constructively, acknowledge this change. Celebrate the small victories where your inner dialogue was more supportive and encouraging.

6. Continuous Education: View this process as a journey of lifelong learning. Just as a good leadership style requires constant reflection and adjustment, transforming your inner critic into a supportive mentor requires ongoing attention and fine-tuning.

7. Practice Empathy Towards Yourself: Train your inner critic to empathize with your feelings and experiences. Just as a compassionate leader strives to understand their team members' perspectives, your inner critic should learn to appreciate your challenges and emotions. This empathetic approach can soften the criticism and make it more constructive.

8. Role Play Scenarios: Engage in mental role-play exercises where your inner critic plays the role of a supportive mentor during challenging situations. Visualize scenarios where you might typically be hard on yourself and practice how your transformed inner critic would offer guidance and encouragement instead.

11. Create an Inner Boardroom: Imagine your inner critic as one of many advisors in an internal boardroom. Invite other, more supportive voices to join, such as your inner cheerleader, realist, and problem-solver. This way, when your inner critic speaks up, it's balanced by other perspectives, encouraging a more holistic and constructive internal dialogue.

12. Set Specific Improvement Goals: Instead of vague criticisms, have your inner critic set specific, achievable goals for improvement. This turns criticism into a roadmap for personal growth and development, making the feedback from your inner critic more actionable and less about personal failure.

13. Journaling for Perspective: Keep a journal where you write down instances of criticism from your inner critic and then reframe them from the perspective of a mentor. This exercise can help solidify the transformation of your inner critic into a source of constructive advice.

By sending your inner critic to leadership training, you're not eliminating it—since criticism can indeed be productive when used correctly—but transforming it into a supportive part of your inner world that contributes to personal growth and development.

18. "NO" IS A COMPLETE SEN-TENCE. REALLY?

This oft-quoted saying is, in principle, correct but puts especially polite people under a lot of pressure. However, it's not forbidden to build a bridge and embellish the "No" diplomatically with constructive solutions.

Diplomacy Makes Saying "No" Easier

Thomas often feels pressured to meet the expectations of his colleagues and friends. At the same time, he is practicing not neglecting his own needs and setting boundaries. But this is still not easy for him.

When a colleague, Stefan, asks him for last-minute help with a project that needs to be completed by the end of the day, Thomas feels overwhelmed. He remembers the advice that "No" is a complete sentence and decides to act on it this time. "No, I can't," Thomas responds tersely, hoping to maintain his boundaries.

Stefan's facial expression immediately changes from hopeful to disappointed and irritated. The atmosphere between them noticeably cools. Thomas feels guilty and uncomfortable because, although he has maintained his boundaries, he feels he has jeopardized an important relationship.

He had not considered that his brief "No" without further explanation or an offer of support could be interpreted as a lack of willingness to cooperate or even as a rejection.

To constructively shape such situations, Thomas could have accompanied his "No" with a solution approach. For example, he could have said, "Stefan, I understand that this project is important, and I would really like to help. Unfortunately, I have a tight deadline myself today and can't fully focus on it. But let's see if we can find someone else on the team who has the capacity. Or, if there's time until tomorrow, I can help you then."

This approach would have several advantages:

1. Showing understanding: By expressing his understanding of Stefan's situation, the emotional connection remains intact.

2. Setting boundaries: Thomas clarifies his current boundaries without appearing rude or distant.

3. Offering solutions: He shows willingness to support by suggesting alternatives, either by referring to another colleague or by offering to help at a later time.

By communicating a "No" in this way, relationships can be nurtured and strengthened, even when one is unable to fulfill immediate requests. It creates a bridge of understanding and cooperation that can pave the way for future collaboration without neglecting one's own boundaries and needs.

But how do you learn this? What solutions are available? How can you compile a portfolio from which you can choose as needed and garnish your "no"? Here are some possible steps I've compiled for you:

Step 1: Self-reflection and preparation

Start with a self-reflection on your past experiences of declining requests. Think about situations where you found it difficult to say "No" and analyze what the challenge was. Were it fears about the relationship with the other person, lack of self-confidence, or the fear of being perceived as unhelpful?

Prepare by clearly defining your boundaries and priorities. What's important to you and where do you need to set boundaries to protect your energy and resources?

This helps you to make quicker and clearer decisions in future situations about whether and how you can decline a request.

Step 2: Developing a solutions portfolio

Create a "portfolio" of solution options that you can use depending on the situation. This could include:

1. Alternative time suggestions: If you can't help now, offer specific alternative times.

2. Referring to other resources: Recommend books, websites, or colleagues who could also be helpful.

3. Partial support: If you can't provide full help, offer to take on a part of the request that fits into your schedule.

4. Offering a follow-up: Suggest revisiting the situation at a later time to see if you can then provide support.

Step 3: Deepen Communication training

Enhancing your communication skills is crucial for effectively conveying your "No" with diplomatic solutions. Role-playing with friends or colleagues serves as a practical method, allowing you to navigate and adapt to a variety of responses. This practice enables you to explore different scenarios and refine your approach, ensuring you remain respectful yet assertive.

Consider incorporating the following strategies into your role-playing exercises:

1. Empathetic Listening: Before responding, truly listen to what the other person is saying. This helps in understanding their perspective and formulating a response that acknowledges their needs while still maintaining your boundaries.

2. Clear and Concise Language: Use straightforward language that leaves little room for misinterpretation. Be assertive in your delivery, ensuring your message is understood as intended.

3. Body Language and Tone: Pay attention to your body language and tone of voice. Non-verbal cues can significantly impact how your message is received. A calm and open demeanor can help mitigate potential defensiveness from the other party.

4. Use "I" Statements: Articulate your responses with "I" statements to express how you feel and what you need without placing blame. For example, instead of saying, "You're overloading me with tasks," try, "I feel overwhelmed with the current workload and need to prioritize my tasks."

5. Prepare for Pushback: In some scenarios, your "No" may not be readily accepted. Practice how to remain firm in your stance without becoming aggressive or yielding under pressure.

6. Feedback Mechanism: After each role-playing session, ask for honest feedback on your communication style, choice of words, and overall demeanor. Use this feedback to improve and adjust your approach accordingly.

This in-depth communication training not only prepares you to handle immediate situations where you need to say "No" but also equips you with lifelong skills for assertive and respectful interactions in both personal and professional contexts.

Step 4: Practicing self-compassion

Remember that it's normal to have difficulties when declining requests, and that every situation is an opportunity to learn and grow. Be gentle with yourself and recognize the courage it takes to set boundaries.

By learning to communicate your "No" constructively and developing a portfolio of solution options, you not only strengthen your own boundaries but also foster healthy, respectful relationships with others.

Step 8: Assertive Training

Enroll in assertive communication training or workshops. These can equip you with the skills to express your refusal in a way that is both clear and respectful, minimizing the potential for misunderstanding or conflict.

Also, find a mentor who excels in assertive communication and boundary-setting. Their guidance and insight can be invaluable as you navigate the complexities of saying "No" in various contexts. By incorporating these steps, you further refine your ability to say "No" in a manner that maintains respect and empathy for both parties involved. It's about balancing kindness with assertiveness, ensuring that you honor your own needs while still considering those of others.

19: DON'T FEAR ROLE-PLAYING

Role-playing is one of the most powerful tools when it comes to practicing difficult new behaviors like saying "No."

An Illustrative Example

Lena faced a challenge that many of us may find familiar: she was repeatedly asked for favors she didn't want or couldn't fulfill but found it incredibly hard to say "No."

Each time such a situation arose, she felt caught between a rock and a hard place – wanting to be helpful and supportive on one hand, but feeling her own boundaries being crossed and resources drained on the other.

One day, she shared her dilemma with her friend Jana over coffee. Jana suggested using role-playing as a method to help Lena get better at saying "No."

Initially, Lena was skeptical. The idea of simulating a conversation where she had to deny someone's request seemed almost as uncomfortable as the real situation. But Jana convinced her to at least give it a try.

They started with a simple scene: Jana played a colleague asking Lena to help with a project over the weekend that wasn't Lena's responsibility.

Initially, Lena responded as she always did – with a hesitant "Yes," which she immediately regretted. But after a few runs and with Jana's encouragement, Lena began to find and express alternative answers.

They practiced various scenarios, from small favors among friends to larger requests at work.

With each repetition, Lena felt more secure. She learned to find her own voice and clearly, yet kindly, communicate her needs. Role-playing gave her the chance to try different strategies and see the reactions to them without the fear of real consequences. It was as if she had entered a protected space where she could practice without fear of judgment.

This experience was a turning point for Lena. Not only did she learn a lot about herself in the role-plays, but she also realized that saying "No" didn't have to mean the end of a relationship but was a way to preserve her own boundaries while still being respectful.

When she was asked for an inappropriate favor in the real world again, Lena still felt a flutter in her stomach.

But this time, it was different. She took a deep breath, remembered her practice with Jana, and said "No" clearly and firmly, followed by a suggestion on how she could help differently.

To her surprise, her "No" was accepted, the relationship remained intact, and Lena felt stronger and more confident than ever before.

This simple but transformative experience with role-playing not only taught Lena how to effectively say "No" but also opened a new path to assertiveness and personal development.

Why Do Role-Plays Work?

Role-playing is much more than an exercise – it's a powerful self-improvement tool and a guide for personal growth. It allows us to experiment, learn, and grow within a safe framework.

Let's explore the psychological reasons behind the effectiveness of role-plays:

1. Learning Through Experience: Psychology teaches us that experiential learning is among the most effective forms of learning. Role-plays allow us to experience and navigate situations before they occur in the real world. This "rehearsal" not only builds knowledge but also boosts confidence in our abilities.

2. Self-Mirror: Role-plays act as a mirror, enabling us to see ourselves from a new perspective. By observing our behavior and reactions in simulated scenarios, we can recognize and understand unconscious patterns that influence our daily lives.

3. Emotional Safety: The risk of negative consequences is significantly reduced in a role-play. This emotional safety grants us the freedom to try new behaviors and cross boundaries we might not dare in regular life.

4. Empathy and Perspective-Taking: By putting ourselves in others' shoes, we develop a deeper understanding and empathy for their feelings and reactions. This change in perspective is essential for improving interpersonal relationships and communication skills.

5. Anxiety Reduction: Often, the biggest hurdle in saying "No" is the fear of negative consequences. Role-plays help mitigate this fear by creating a risk-free environment where mistakes can be made and learned from without fearing real-world repercussions.

6. Increased Self-Assurance: Repeated practice in role-plays enhances self-assurance in our ability to set boundaries and communicate our needs. This confidence is crucial when faced with real-life challenges.

7. Constructive Feedback: Role-plays provide the opportunity to receive immediate feedback from play partners or observers. This feedback can be immensely valuable in refining your technique and becoming more effective.

Role-plays offer a unique chance to experiment and learn in a safe and controlled environment.

They allow us to play out various scenarios, anticipate reactions, and hone our communication skills before applying them in real situations.

This is especially valuable when learning and solidifying difficult behaviors like declining requests.

How To: Practical Implementation of Role-Plays

Role-playing is a potent tool for practicing and perfecting difficult new behaviors. But how do you start?

Here's a sort of "how-to" guide for those who want to try role-playing but aren't sure how to begin:

1. Prepare Scenarios: Start by creating a list of situations where you feel uncomfortable or have difficulty saying "No." This can range from work scenarios to family requests to social obligations.

2. Find a Role-Play Partner: Look for a friend, family member, or colleague you trust and who is willing to practice with you. It might also be helpful to choose someone who wants to improve their behavior in similar situations so you can learn from each other.

3. Switch Roles: Alternate roles so that each participant has the chance to be both the person saying "No" and the one making the request. This enhances understanding and the ability to empathize with others.

4. Reflect and Adjust: After each role-play session, take time to reflect on the experience. Discuss what went well and what could be improved. Be open to feedback and ready to adjust your approach.

5. Seek Feedback: Once you start to communicate your "No" constructively, ask for feedback from people you trust. How was your "No" received? Were there positive changes in how others reacted to your rejections?

6. Reflect and Adjust: Regularly reflect on your experiences. What worked well, and what could be improved?

Adjust your portfolio of solution options accordingly and be open to new strategies.

7. Practice Self-Compassion: Remember that it's normal to struggle with declining requests, and every situation presents a learning and growth opportunity. Be kind to yourself and recognize the courage it takes to set boundaries.

8. Incorporate Feedback: Use feedback from your role-play partner to refine your approach. If certain phrases or tactics are particularly effective, make a note to use them in real situations.

9. Expand Your Scenarios: As you become more comfortable with role-playing, expand your scenarios to include more complex or challenging situations. This will help you build resilience and adaptability.

10. Practice Regularly: Like any skill, saying "No" confidently takes practice. Regular role-playing sessions can help you fine-tune your approach and become more comfortable with setting boundaries.

11. Use Visualizations: Alongside role-playing, practice visualizing yourself successfully saying "No" in various situations. This mental rehearsal can reinforce your ability to act confidently in real life.

12. Celebrate Progress: Recognize and celebrate your progress, no matter how small. Each successful role-play or real-life application of saying "No" is a step towards stronger boundaries and increased self-confidence.

By learning to communicate your "No" constructively and developing a portfolio of solution options, you not only strengthen your own boundaries but also foster healthy, respectful relationships with others.

Want more? Try an Advanced Acting Course

And here's a hot tip for everyone who has discovered role-playing not just as an exercise but as a path to personal development: specialized acting classes offer an even deeper opportunity.

Such courses, led by experienced acting coaches, are designed to work on themes like self-confidence, assertiveness, and sovereignty in small groups. They use theater techniques to help participants refine their expression, strengthen their presence, and communicate more effectively with others.

This type of instruction goes beyond traditional role-playing and delves deeper into the art of performance. It's an opportunity to experiment in a supportive environment, take on various roles, and thus explore different facets of one's personality.

Participants learn to use body language consciously, effectively use their voice, and authentically convey their emotions.

All these skills are valuable not only on stage but also in everyday life, especially in professional contexts or situations that require a high degree of self-assurance.

Participating in such acting classes can be a transformative experience. Many find not only a new form of assertiveness here but also discover a new understanding of themselves and a novel sovereignty in shaping their relationships and interactions with the world.

It's an opportunity to overcome fears, expand boundaries, and fully tap into one's potential.

So, if you enjoy role-playing and are looking for further ways to enhance your communicative abilities and self-confidence, such specialized acting classes might be just right for you.

It's an investment in yourself that goes far beyond the classical understanding of acting and can have profound effects on your personal and professional life.

20. SAYING "NO" LIKE AN ACTOR

There's a great way to lose the fear of the moment of saying "no": Just imagine you're playing a role in a play.

Playing a role makes it less personal

At the end of the last chapter, I already introduced the possibility of attending a specialized acting course, which experienced actors occasionally offer for "ordinary people." For those who want to learn to appear more confident and sovereign with the means of acting, to assert themselves better, or just to learn more about themselves.

In this chapter, I want to suggest something that you can also learn in such an acting course, but which you can also apply and practice here and today: If you have problems with your "no," simply play it like an actor plays their role.

Why is this approach so effective?

This approach of playing the "no" like a good actor is based on a strong psychological foundation: distancing.

When we play a role, we create a mental distance between our true self and the situation we're in.

This distance allows us to react less emotionally and personally to potentially stressful or conflict-ridden situations. We give ourselves permission to act differently than we might normally do, free from the burden of self-criticism and the fear of negative judgments.

By taking on a role, we can build an emotional distance from the situation. This distance helps us to be less vulnerable to rejection or criticism. By pretending to be someone else who can say "no" confidently and decisively, we lessen the intensity of our own fears and self-doubts.

Playing a role also allows for greater flexibility in our reactions. We can experiment with different behaviors and find out which strategies are most effective without it having direct effects on our self-image. This willingness to experiment can lead to more effective and creative solutions for setting boundaries.

And over time, playing a confident, decisive role causes these qualities to carry over into our actual self-behavior. Similar to the "fake it till you make it" method, the repeated portrayal of self-assurance and sovereignty can strengthen our confidence in real situations.

Moreover, by playing a role, we implicitly also use the technique of learning through observation. We imagine how a confident person would act in a situation and imitate these actions. This form of learning is particularly powerful because it allows us to experience ourselves as competent and capable, which in turn can positively influence our self-concept.

The psychological foundation

The psychological foundation of this approach is deeply rooted in the theory of social learning and cognitive behavioral therapy. Both disciplines emphasize the importance of learned behaviors through imitation and the power of cognitive restructuring - changing our thought patterns to influence our behavior.

By playing a role, we use these mechanisms to acquire new, constructive behaviors and transform our self-image.

This approach thus provides a powerful method not only to change our behavior in specific situations but also to improve our general self-confidence and self-perception. It teaches us that we don't have to be victims of our fears and insecurities but that we can take control of our reactions and emotions through conscious action and a little creative role-playing.

Exercise Guide: Saying "No" Like an Actor

And how do you start if you want to try this method? Here's a clear guide:

1. Choose a role: Start by selecting a role or character you want to represent. This could be a fictional character from a book or film, a historical figure known for their decisiveness, or even an idealized version of yourself - someone who can set boundaries confidently, calmly, and sovereignly.

2. Character study: Spend some time studying your character. What makes this person (or ideal version of you) so confident and decisive? How do they stand, how do they speak, what gestures do they use? The more detailed you can imagine these attributes, the better.

3. Prepare a script: Prepare a short "script" that includes typical situations where you have difficulty saying "no." Write an appropriate response for each situation that your character would give. Make sure these responses not only include a clear "no" but also the tone and posture you've envisioned for your character.

4. Role-play: Conduct a role-play where you take on your chosen role. You can do this alone in front of a mirror or ask a friend to play the part of the other person in your script. Make sure to practice not just the words but also imitate the body language and tone of your character.

5. Reflection: After conducting the role-play, take a moment for a short reflection. How did you feel stepping into the role? Were there differences in your feeling of self-assurance or in your ability to say "no"? Which elements of the role-play could you implement in real situations?

6. Integration into daily life: Start integrating elements of your role-play into daily life. Maybe start with situations that are less threatening, and slowly work your way up to more difficult scenarios. Remember, it's not about being someone else permanently but using tools and techniques to help you act more confidently

7. Continuous practice: Like any skill, continuous practice is key. Regularly repeat the role-plays, vary the scenarios, and adjust your script based on new insights or situations. The more you practice, the more naturally you'll be able to incorporate this new, confident way of saying "no" into your behavior.

This exercise guide is designed to help you master the art of saying "no" by utilizing acting techniques. It's a creative and effective method to not only strengthen your communication skills but also boost your self-confidence and develop a deeper understanding of your own boundaries.

21. CRYSTAL CLEAR RATHER THAN INDIRECT

Many people say "no" so softly and cautiously that it can't even be recognized as a "no." Thus, they endure all the mental stress of overcoming themselves, but still, the desired outcome is not achieved.

Clear and Direct Beats Vague

Tom and Julia faced a common problem, but approached it in different ways. Both were known for always being helpful—a trait that, of course, made them very popular in the eyes of their colleagues and friends. However, this willingness to help also meant they were often inundated with requests and favors that demanded more of their time and energy than was feasible.

One day, Tom was asked by a colleague to help out with a project that wasn't really part of his responsibilities. He actually wanted to say "no," as he was already under a lot of work pressure.

But out of fear of appearing rude, he worded his refusal so indirectly and softly that his colleague thought Tom would agree. "I'm pretty swamped at the moment, but maybe I'll find some time later, I'll just see...," Tom said in a tone that conveyed more hope than refusal. The result: The colleague assumed Tom was on board and planned with his support.

Julia experienced a similar situation when a friend asked her to help organize a party. Although Julia knew she didn't have the time, she feared disappointing her friend.

So, she said in a hesitant tone: "Well, I'll have to see, but I'm not quite sure if I can make it, I already have quite a lot on my plate..."

Her friend only heard the possibility of a "yes" and did not perceive Julia's hesitation as a clear refusal.

Both Tom and Julia experienced the mental stress of wanting to assert a "no," without their actual intention—a clear "no"—being understood.

They realized that their indirect way of communicating not only led to misunderstandings but also increased their own burden without ultimately setting the boundaries they intended to.

Following these experiences, they decided to adopt a different approach. They resolved to communicate clearly and directly, without being rude.

In a shared role-play, they practiced how to choose their words and adjust their tone to avoid misunderstandings. "I understand you need help, and I'm sorry, but I can't assist at the moment," became their new mantra. They practiced standing firm and confident, maintaining eye contact, and expressing their "nos" with convincing clarity.

The next time Tom and Julia were faced with similar situations, they were prepared. Their clear and direct way of communicating led to their decisions being respected without damaging relationships. They found that the clarity of their communication not only avoided misunderstandings but also strengthened their self-confidence.

Exercises in Clear Communication

To learn clear communication and to effectively say "no," the following exercises can help:

1. Self-reflection: Take time to think about past situations where your "no" was not clear enough. Ask yourself what held you back from being more direct. Write down your thoughts and feelings about it.

2. Positive Formulation of Boundaries: Practice formulating your boundaries positively. Instead of saying: "I can't do that because...," try: "I'm currently focusing on other priorities and cannot fulfill your request."

3. Role-plays with friends or family: Yes, we've discussed role-plays often in this book. But it really does work... So, conduct role-plays with someone you trust where you need to say "no." Start with less challenging scenarios and gradually increase the difficulty. Ask for feedback on your clarity and directness.

4. Tone and Body Language: Practice your tone and body language in front of a mirror when saying "no." Ensure you appear firm yet friendly. Eye contact, an upright posture, and a calm voice support the clarity of your message.

5. "No" without justification: While I've extensively explained in Chapter 16 why it's usually better to diplomatically embellish a "no," this exercise serves its purpose as such: try saying "no" without justifying yourself. Start with everyday situations, like declining a salesperson. This helps overcome the feeling of needing to justify. Diplomacy is optional and desirable, but not a necessity;

it's purely a courtesy and kindness from you! This exercise helps you internalize this.

6. Use Clear Language: Ensure you use clear and unambiguous words. Avoid vague, weakening filler words like "maybe" or "somehow," which could dilute your message. Practice sentences like: "I understand your standpoint, but my decision is..."

7. Set Communication Boundaries: Aim to consciously set boundaries in every communication at least once. This can be in both professional and personal settings. Reflect afterward on how it went and what you could improve next time.

8. Prepare for difficult conversations: If you know a tough conversation is coming, prepare. Write down what you want to say and practice it. Good preparation gives you confidence and helps articulate your thoughts clearly and directly.

9. Seek Positive Reinforcement: Note down situations where your clear communication was positively received. Celebrate these successes and how they made you feel. This positive reinforcement motivates and affirms you on your path to clear and direct communication.

These exercises support you in enhancing your ability to communicate clearly and master saying "no," leading to more respectful and healthier relationships.

Phrasing Assistance for Your "No"

Here is a comprehensive, albeit far from exhaustive, list of phrasing examples showing how to say "no" clearly, kindly, and diplomatically:

1. Direct, yet gentle: "I really appreciate your request, but I cannot commit at the moment."

2. Offering an alternative: "Unfortunately, I can't help with this project. Have you spoken to [Name]? He/She might be the right person for it."

3. Right timing: "This week is already fully booked for me. Could we push this to next week?"

4. Expressing gratitude: "Thank you for your offer/trust. Sadly, it doesn't fit into my schedule right now."

5. Setting boundaries: "To concentrate on my current commitments, I have to say no."

6. Open for the future: "I can't engage with this right now, but let's revisit it later."

7. Honest and respectful: "I'm honored that you thought of me, but I have to be realistic about my capacities and decline."

8. Short and sweet: "I can't take this on, but thanks for asking."

9. Positive spin: "I'm currently focusing on [a specific task/ project], so I can't commit."

10. Confident and firm: "I have to pass this time. Thanks for your understanding."

11. Considering personal needs: "To meet my own deadlines, I have to say no."

12. Clarifying priorities: "I need to stick to my priorities and can't take on new projects at the moment."

13. Empathetic refusal: "I understand how important this is to you, and it's hard for me to say no, but I can't provide the support needed right now."

14. Unambiguous: "Unfortunately, no, but I wish you the best with it."

15. Sharing responsibility: "I can't handle it alone, but if we can assemble a team, I'd be willing to contribute a part."

16. Offering a compromise: "I can't take on the entire project, but I could handle specific tasks. How does that sound to you?"

17. Asking for time to consider: "Please let me think it over, and I'll get back to you tomorrow." (Make sure you actually do get back to them.)

18. Focus on solution: "I'm not the best person for this task. Perhaps you can find the support you need from [alternative solution/resource]."

19. Connecting refusal with a question: "Could someone else who might have more capacity right now take this on?"

20. Diplomatic and clear: "I need to focus on my core projects, so it's not possible for me to take this on."

These phrases help you say "no" while staying respectful and positive, yet firmly maintaining your boundaries.

Pick the ones that suit you best, memorize them like a script, and then practice them in as many situations as possible.

And expand the list with items and examples that fit your requirements and individual situation. This list primarily includes examples from a professional context. If your focus is more on personal life, for instance, if you need to set boundaries with a dominant sibling or a friend who often crosses lines, feel free to customize the list accordingly. After working through this book, you should have the tools needed to tackle such issues independently.

22. MOTIVATIO-NAL LETTERS TO YOURSELF

At any point of learning a new skill, setbacks are inevitable. It's great to have someone to remind you why you started in the first place and to motivate you to keep going. That someone can be yourself.

Letters from Good Phases for Bad Phases

Laura set a goal to become a better public speaker, knowing it was crucial for her career as a marketing specialist. Her initial steps on this path were promising. She attended workshops, practiced in front of the mirror, and even sought opportunities to speak at team meetings. Each success left her feeling invincible and fulfilled.

In these moments of euphoria and pride, she wrote letters to herself, documenting her progress, determination, and joy in overcoming her fears.

However, like any learning process, there were setbacks. There were days when her presentations didn't go as planned. Once, she even received direct, harsh feedback from a colleague that shook her confidence.

During these moments of self-doubt and frustration, Laura found it difficult to remember the positive feelings of her successes. The memory of why she had started seemed far away.

At one of these low points, she remembered the letters she had written to herself during better times. Reluctantly, she pulled out the first letter she wrote after her very first successful workshop.

Reading the lines about how proud she was of herself for overcoming her fear and looking forward to continuing to grow, she felt her perspective begin to shift. The letter reminded her that setbacks are part of the growth process and that she had the ability and strength to overcome them.

With each letter read, Laura's resolve grew. The words she wrote when she was highly motivated and full of energy now gave her the strength not to give up.

They reminded her that she had started out of passion and that every setback ultimately brought her closer to her goal. The letters became a source of inspiration and comfort, reminding her why she had embarked on her journey in the first place.

Through this experience, Laura learned how powerful motivational letters to oneself can be. She made it a regular practice to write letters after significant successes and positive moments to create a collection of motivational messages for difficult times.

These letters not only helped her navigate the lows of her journey but also became a valuable archive of her personal development and successes.

How to Start This Powerful Tool Most Effectively

To begin with the effective technique of motivational letters to yourself and build it effectively, follow this step-by-step guide:

1. Choose the Right Moment: Start by writing letters in moments of joy, pride, or contentment. These moments can occur after a personal achievement, at the end of a fulfilling day, or simply during a phase when you feel particularly motivated. Capture this moment when you are positively attuned and have a clear vision of your path.

2. Choose Your Medium: Decide whether you want to write your letters by hand or digitally. Handwritten letters can have a more personal touch, and reading them later can be a more intimate experience. Digital letters, however, are easier to store and retrieve when needed. Whatever you choose, ensure it's convenient and accessible for you.

3. Be Honest and Open: When writing, be as open and honest as possible. These letters are for you, so don't hesitate to share your true feelings, hopes, and dreams. Describe what you have achieved, how you felt about it, and why it's important to you.

4. Compose Motivational Messages: Write encouraging words to your future self. These could be reminders of how far you've come, affirmations of your abilities, or simply positive affirmations for the times you'll need them most.

5. Give Specific Examples: Mention specific challenges you've overcome and how you managed to do so. This will serve as evidence of your strength and resilience during difficult times.

6. Establish a Safe Storage Place: Find a safe and special place to store your letters. This could be a box, a folder, or a special directory on your computer. The place should be personally meaningful and easily accessible when you need a motivational boost.

7. Schedule Regular Reviews: Set times when you want to review your letters. This could be once a year, on your birthday, or at the beginning of a new year. You can also decide to read a letter whenever you feel discouraged or face a major challenge.

8. Reflect and Add: When you read a letter, take the time to think about where you stand now compared to when you wrote the letter. Use the opportunity to write more letters capturing your current feelings and experiences.

9. Share If You Wish: Although these letters are primarily for yourself, you can also choose to share them with a trusted friend or family member. This can be a way to get support and also show others how far you've come.

10. Celebrate Progress and Resilience: In each letter, celebrate not just the achievements, but also the resilience and perseverance it took to reach them. Acknowledging the journey and the challenges you've faced reinforces your ability to handle future obstacles.

11. Visualize Future Successes: Use your letters to visualize future achievements and how you plan to reach them. This acts as a commitment to your goals and can be incredibly motivating when you read these predictions and plans in the future, especially when you've achieved them or are on the path to doing so.

12. Incorporate Quotes and Inspirations: Include quotes, sayings, or any external pieces of wisdom that resonate with you. These can serve as powerful reminders and motivational boosts when revisiting your letters.

13. Create a Letter Exchange with Future You: Treat some of your letters as part of an exchange with your future self. Ask questions, express hopes, and then, when you revisit these letters, write responses to these from the perspective of your future self.

14. Set Specific Checkpoints: In your letters, set specific future dates or milestones when you plan to read them. This creates a sense of anticipation and a structured timeline for reflection.

15. Reflect on Personal Growth Themes: Identify themes of personal growth that emerge over time in your letters. This can help you understand deeper patterns in your development and areas where you've made significant progress or need further growth.

16. Integrate Art and Creativity: Don't limit yourself to text. Feel free to include drawings, collages, or any other form of art that expresses your feelings and aspirations.

These creative elements can make the letters more personal and engaging.

17. Address Different Aspects of Your Life: Write letters focusing on different areas of your life, such as career, personal relationships, hobbies, or personal well-being. This holistic approach ensures that you're acknowledging and motivating yourself across the spectrum of your life experiences.

18. Create an Annual Letter Ritual: Make it a tradition to write a comprehensive letter to yourself at the end of each year. Summarize your achievements, the obstacles you've overcome, and set intentions for the coming year.

19. Share the Practice: Encourage friends or family members to start their own practice of writing motivational letters to themselves. Sharing this practice can lead to a supportive community where you inspire and motivate each other.

20. Leave Letters Unopened: Consider writing a letter and leaving it unopened until a future date. The anticipation of reading your own words at a later time can be a unique way to bridge your past and future selves.

By writing motivational letters to yourself, you create a personal archive of self-love, encouragement, and growth that can help you through tough times and remind you of your strengths and successes.

CLOSING WORDS

We have now reached the end of our journey together—a journey aimed at equipping you with tools and techniques to master the art of saying "No". Through the chapters of this book, we've explored the many facets of this seemingly simple yet in reality, profound and often challenging skill.

It's important to emphasize that this book is far from comprehensive. What you've found in these pages is merely a selection of psychotherapeutic techniques and approaches meant to ease your entry and serve as inspiration.

The art of saying "No" is complex and as varied as we humans are. There are countless other methods, perspectives, and personal insights waiting to be discovered on this path.

I want to thank you for your openness and commitment to engaging in this process. It takes courage to recognize, respect, and communicate existing boundaries, and you've taken a significant step towards a self-determined and fulfilled life.

And finally, a request. The feedback that you, the readers, provide, whether through a review or an email, is invaluable. It serves not only as motivation but also as a compass for future works. If this book is well-received and found helpful by my readers, I look forward to writing a sequel.

There's so much more to explore, learn, and share. Your stories, experiences, and what you learn on your journey could form the core of a next book that dives even deeper into the subject. So, please feel free to share it with me!

Until then, I encourage you to continue being brave, stay true to yourself, and utilize and adapt the techniques we've explored together. The journey of saying "No" doesn't end with the last page of this book—it's an ongoing process of growth and self-discovery. Stay strong, stay courageous, and above all: stay true to yourself.

With warmest regards and in great anticipation of our further adventures,

Dr. Barbara Gorißen

ABOUT THE AUTHOR

After passing her board examination in Internal Medicine in Germany, Dr. med. Barbara Gorißen worked as an emergency physician and head emergency physician for over ten years, during which time she also pursued intensive further education in medical hypnotherapy and psychotherapy.

Having obtained the additional qualification in psychotherapy from the Hesse Chamber of Physicians, she established her private practice and has since been working as a psychotherapist and author. Her focus topics are depression, burnout, fears, neurodiversity (ADHD, autism, high sensitivity), and introversion.

Also published in English:

Dr. Barbara Gorißen: Over 300 examples of ADHD symptoms. A comprehensive collection from ADHD diagnostics. ISBN 979-8882510663

Printed in Great Britain
by Amazon